Street Singing and Preaching

Other Books by Martin Bell

The Way of the Wolf
Nenshu and the Tiger
Return of the Wolf
Night Places
Distant Fire
Wolf

STREET SINGING & PREACHING

A Book of New Psalms

Martin Bell

ABINGDON PRESS/ *Nashville*

STREET SINGING AND PREACHING:
A BOOK OF NEW PSALMS

Copyright © 1991 by Martin Bell

This book is printed on recycled, acid-free paper.

Library of Congress Cataloging-in-Publication Data

Bell, Martin, 1937–
    Street singing and preaching : a book of new psalms / Martin Bell.
        p.   cm.
    ISBN 0-687-39965-3 (alk. paper)
    1. Meditations.   I. Title.
BV4832.2.B415   1991
242'.8—dc20   91-12717
                                                   CIP

For John Paul Mussleman

Foreword

Martin Bell knows a lot about faith, having lived to the depths and soared to the heights. He knows a lot about human yearnings that are marked by awe, restlessness, dread, and delight. He loves words and knows what to do to make faith palpable and human life livable.

Religious poetry may be a little like liturgic dance, with only a few basic movements, "two of these, and two of these." The art is working those few options with freshness, daring, and healing. Bell's poetry is not unlike liturgic dance. We are led to the edge of our rational discernment, and then slightly beyond with an awed gasp. His phrases are like a cascade in which newness tumbles out, so quick and so crafted. It comes in phrases like "rafter-rattling praise," "cold web of sin," "luminous, destinal journey," and "at the bottom of the pit is the rule of God." Nothing here that is tired or trite or predictable. Through such an offer as this is the way morning breaks "fresh from the word," fresh beyond despair too deep and fresh beyond certitude too sure.

Walter Brueggemann
Columbia Theological Seminary

Contents

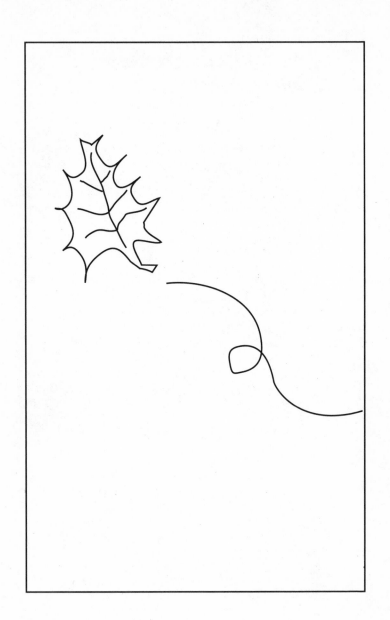

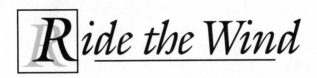

Ride the Wind

Give honor to Yahweh, all creation! Testify to the
   radiant power of God!
Let the hearts of the unspeaking speak, and the vision
   of the unseeing be told!
Let the ears of the unhearing resound with eternal,
   symphonic praise! Let those who are broken and
   lame rise up to embrace the wondering world!

Because it is Yahweh who cares for the abused and
   forgotten ones; with holy bread the Almighty
   blesses a starving people.
Every creature finds shelter under the wings of God, and
   the courts of Yahweh bestow justice on the poor.
Wisdom clears a path for the traveler, and makes
   beautiful the appearance of every dying leaf.

Before all beginnings, God spoke the cosmogonic
   Word, and Yahweh's faithfulness gave birth to
   mortality.
As mother, father, and midwife, the Ruler of All took
   nothing and shaped the breathing membrane of
   creation.
Deep space coruscated with stars.

Threads of pure energy stretched and contracted,
     sweeping the heavens clean.
Like silent dancers, the galaxies swirled in majestic
     circles, escorted by dark, mysterious cosmic
     matter.
Then Creator God sanctified the visible and the
     invisible; Yahweh empowered the living and the
     dying, making covenant with all that had been
     worded into existence.

Who will unlock the riddle of the skies? Will
     humankind view a galaxy from beyond space, or
     succeed in controlling its rotation?
Can a cube of interstellar gas be studied, or a neutron
     star dissected? Will death deign to share its secrets
     with the living?

Confronted by the Enabling Word, mortal empires
     stagger and careen; they cannot stand against the
     headwind of God.
The Lover of Justice lays seige to oppression, and
     issues God's challenge to the power-brokers.
In glass-wrapped buildings they will find no safety, no
     hiding place from the eye of God.

Though the poor are wounded and shattered, the
     Source of All will not forget them.
While tyrants hide their faces in the dust, the castaways
     and exiles and hopeless ones will shine with
     immortal glory.

Surrounded by the groaning, expectant wind of desert
consciousness, we await God's deliverance.
Our trust is in the Sovereign One, whose Word howls
and heaves everywhere within the wild and
radiant universe.

Give honor to Redeemer God, who takes the measure
of infinity and assuages the torment of the
helpless.
Give honor to Yahweh, all creation.

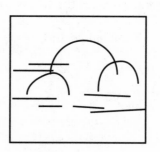

Abraham Lives! Sarah Lives!

*T*he wicked claim they have discarded God; they
  travel on streams of death.
They speak empty words into the emptiness, using
  falsehood to conceal their inner decay.
Competition seduces men and women alike; it
  condemns the unlikely and unworthy to hell.
Disciples of progress ignore God's radiant promise;
  they run as though trying to outrun death.

Hear the testimony of Moses: Yahweh our God is God
  of the living!
The Holy One makes covenant with a living people;
  the Giver of Peace lays ultimate claim to creation.
We announce to all: Abraham did not perish, and
  Sarah did not perish; they are alive unto the living
  God.
Rebecca and Isaac are not dead, they are not dead,
  Lord; nor were Jacob and Rachel abandoned to
  darkness.
These are the living children of Yahweh, and they
  travel in a realm ablaze with angels!

This is the witness of faith: No physical decay, no
     earthly power can cancel the promise of God.
Yahweh's covenant dispels the winding sheet of
     mortality; Wisdom banishes death like an animal
     shaking water off its back.

Humanity cannot find God; the Holy One it is who
     pursues and retrieves every creature.
Yahweh presents each one with a covenant already
     signed, a promise etched into the universe.
When our spirits shrivel, when depression overtakes us,
     we are recalled to life by the steadfast love of God.
Fierce, brooding grace breaks through estrangement;
     Wisdom shatters the structures built by sin.

Yahweh is God of the living: the free God, the
     Uncontainable One.
Yahweh is God of all the saints who have gone before,
     of the great cloud of witnesses who sustain us in
     our pain and in our loneliness.
God is eternally bound to creation; the Holy One
     carries us like a mother carrying in her arms an
     injured child.

Paradoxes of dust and of dreams, we place our trust in
     you, O Lord; do not abandon us to the gods of
     consumption.
Save us from the temptations of earthly security,
     deliver us from the demons of opulence.
Let the world resound with good news, the good news
     of God's redemption! Hallelujah!

The covenant cannot be broken and the covenant will
	not be broken! Abraham lives and Sarah lives!
And we, too, shall live in the glory-embrace of God!
	Rebecca lives and Isaac lives!
The Ruler of History has made a living pledge with
	creation! Jacob lives and Rachel lives!
And as time dissolves into the rainbows of eternity, the
	universe shouts: It is Yahweh who saves!
	Hallelujah! Hallelujah!

Runaway

I am like a beggar in the streets, like a runaway child
caught in a web of abuse.
Surely, O God, you will not pass me by; you will not
count me worthless.
Your ear, O Holy One, hears the cry of the least of
your creatures; you have chosen the humble and
downcast for your very own.
With wild audacity I call upon you, the Ruler of Time
and Space: Do not withhold your presence from
one who is troubled beyond endurance.

All the world knows my fault; guilt has scarred both
body and spirit.
You have seen the plight of your servant, O Unseen
Power, and you know the condition of my heart.
I come before you, O Sovereign God, without
reservation; ravaged and hurt, I have no defense
except your covenant-promise.
Because you have forgiven, I dare to confess; because
you have canceled my iniquity, I have the courage
to hope.
My hope springs from the Ground of Being, my
confidence from the history of a forgiven people.

The testimony is this: Yahweh our God is eternally
>bound, bound to creation in spite of sin; in spite
>of loneliness and atrocity, injustice and pain.
Yahweh our God chose the universe into being, and
>the Lord decreed an everlasting bond with all that
>was made.
My hope arises from covenant-promise, my confidence
>from the One who protects the world like a
>defiant mother bear.

O my people, do not turn away from God. Do not
>trust in human strength, or in your own
>competitive edge.
Stand vulnerable before the Mystery, the Lord of Life.
>Surely we will see the splendor of new possibility
>appear like sudden lightning.
Shout from radio towers and churches and cornfields:
>God is with us. As blessing and judgment and
>living presence, Yahweh is with us.
God hears the wretched cries of every forsaken
>creature. And God has brought each one safely
>across the Red Sea.
And each one will be carried safely across the barrier of
>death, and each one is safeheld in the profound
>forever-embrace of Yahweh our God.

Waiting Room

*U*pon the ashes of humanity, we dance, we weep.
Our songs are desperate and weary: cacophonies of
    hope betrayed and dreams gone wrong.
In the glare of television spotlights, our leaders
    announce the death of the planet; they say we are
    sealed with the sign of the mushroom cloud.
Like a wall of fire across the earth, hatred makes
    insidious progress; evil is loose of all restraint.

Why do you turn from your people, O Lord? Why
    have you cast us away like garbage?
Remember, O Mother of Creation, how you wrapped
    the world in swaddling clothes, how you
    cherished it with covenant-love.
Do not withhold your blessing from us; look with
    compassion on our withering hope.

Your enemies use famine as a weapon in their civil
    wars; the flesh of the powerless is bruised and
    bleeding.
Displaced by foreign armies, citizens become refugees;
    they inhabit villages solid with tents; innocent
    children are robbed of land and dignity.

Those who speak against oppression are seized;
    wearing neckbands of iron, they are brought
    before the emperors of order.
Unexplained deaths are called suicides, bodies are
    buried in quicksand.

Each spinning of the earth reveals fresh cruelties, new
    and savage desecrations of the innocent.
Entire peoples are targeted for extinction; they are
    carried off in railroad cars and pick-up trucks and
    panel vans.
Like currency concealed in secret bank accounts,
    war-machines are stockpiled beneath the earth.

Many there are who have been seduced by the rich
    meat of apathy; no longer do they hear human
    bones being broken.
No longer do they notice the imploring eyes of
    children; they pass by beggars as easily as they
    tread on cracks in the sidewalk.
The disabled and the mentally ill are called hopeless;
    poverty is said to be the rightful legacy of the poor.

The future teems with endless destruction; the present
    is consumed in unquenchable rage.
Despots and demagogues hold the world hostage;
    louder than the wind, they recite their creeds.
Why do you allow your name to be defiled, O Holy
    One?

Why does your Word not thunder over the desert, O
    God?

You are Ruler of All, the Alpha and Omega; in your
    hands you hold the power of life and the power of
    death.
You decided the universe into being, and you sowed
    the galaxies in space.
When our forebears passed through the gates of
    slavery, you called them into the realm of faith.
In fire and cloud you revealed yourself. From the lion
    and scorpion you protected them.

Respond now, O God, to the terror of your people; let
    not the vulnerable earth explode into desolation.
Rend the mantle of despair that covers humanity like a
    shroud; uncover the rank decay of human greed.
Do not hide yourself from the helpless ones, or
    abandon those who are strangled by injustice.

Deliver us, O God, from the false promises of empires;
    ransom the children who have been sold into
    necessity.
From crumbling urban wastelands and war-scarred
    lands, gather your scattered people. Do not allow
    your enemies to chisel their claims on the face of
    creation.
Let every forgotten corner be lighted; let the uproar of
    evil finally be silenced.

Sound the trumpet of redemption, O Giver of Peace, so that all might see in a clearer glass, so that all might hear your unfailing Word, so that all might follow the way of Truth.

Nomad

*S*ave me, O Holy One, from the gunfire, and the
stench, and the hatred of brother for brother and
sister for sister.

For seven nights and seven days, O God, I have
cowered amid the rubble.

Seven nights and seven days have I been separated
from my family; in the unquiet darkness of this
hiding place, I utter constant, voiceless prayers.

O Lord of Life, you are the only one who can save me;
your hand alone is able to guide me beyond the
brutal blockades, into a place untarnished by
terror.

Do not absent yourself from this landscape of
devastation, O God; do not fail to rescue your
faithful servant.

Strengthen my frightened, lonely spirit; give safe
harbor to one who has become the pawn of
nations at war.

Save me, O Holy One, from the gunfire, and the
stench, and the hatred of brother for brother and
sister for sister.

We have lived as uprooted weeds, remaining behind
    when our neighbors fled the city of desolation.
The rats grow as large as dogs; they feed on garbage in
    the streets.
Hospitals turn away the sick for lack of medicines; the
    police are powerless—they do no more than
    record the daily carnage.
Like remnants of a lost era, power cables hang from
    splintered wooden poles.

There is no hope except in you, O God, the Giver of
    Life.
Long ago humanity reached the limit of its wisdom;
    now blindness and blood-instinct have replaced
    trust in the Creator of All.
Violence fills the city; now there are craters where
    once were the quiet and shaded parks.
Where once an apartment building gave refuge, there
    remains only a pile of broken concrete.
I am isolated at the center of myself. Except for you,
    my Protector and Defender, I am separated from
    all goodness, all peace, all healing.

Hear my prayer, O God: It was I who sent them to
    cross the border, to escape the murderous snipers
    and the nightly shelling.
My voice spoke loudest in favor of taking the narrow
    road, of risking all in exchange for freedom.

But I have received no word, no message; between
   volleys of shellfire I hear only anonymous
   groanings and the barking of dogs.
Have I sent them to die? Will I find their decaying
   bodies when at last I go to search for food, or
   when it is my turn to escape?
Without them I have nothing; this makeshift bunker
   will be my tomb if you do not deliver me.

Yet even in hell I will not let go of hope; even the
   stones that form my hiding place are alive with
   the energy of your Word.
Though I am imprisoned by chaos, though I am
   victimized by an enemy unseen, yet will I sing the
   story of your mighty acts.
Because you, O Lord, hear every heartbeat; your
   promise is woven in the fabric of creation.
You will shatter the pride of the powerful; their wealth
   shall be soaked in blood, their fine apparel will
   mock them when death approaches with the night
   shadows.

You, O Holy One, give witness to our going out and
   our coming in; you are responsible for the heights
   and for the depths.
Nothing lies beyond your wondrous and triumphant
   grace; no one is excluded from the gift of eternal
   life.

Though soldiers now surround my hiding place, and
birds of prey feed on the dying streets, yet will I
hold fast to your brooding power, O Ruler of
Time and Space.
Surely you will bring me out of the tomb; like a
newborn infant I will bathe in the holy-glory
waters of redemption.

I will tell the dying world of your salvation. My words
shall become resounding songs of praise; they will
reach the farthest corners of earth.
Every creature will know the terrible power of God's
unyielding righteousness: Yahweh our Protector
has routed the destroyers.
Yea, let the destroyers choke on their rage; let them
watch as the downtrodden and the enslaved and
the terrorized ones dance, bounding through the
gates of God's eternal, implacable kingdom.

Tightrope

You, O God, are Sovereign of the Darkness and
   Ruler of the Light. Out of your Word the
   glorious, terrible universe came to be.
Before there was *when*, before there was *where*, you
   spoke. And creation *became:* swirling, exploding,
   contracting.
You decreed the fullness and the void; you worded the
   visible and the invisible.
You, O God, served as midwife to the birthing of the
   stars; your hand scattered the seeds of life across
   infinity:
Planets within solar systems, stars within galaxies, all
   moving like magi across the face of creation.

By thunder and calm your Name is praised, O Giver of
   Peace; both sound and silence worship at your
   table.
In fear and awe, we behold worlds within worlds; we
   ponder one-celled organisms, and fathom the
   velvet depths of space.
How is it that we have walked through the waters and
   have not drowned? What is humanity's role in the
   cosmic drama?

Though we are small and weak, you named us
 caretakers of the planet; into our trembling,
 mortal hands you gave the infant world.
Again and again we fell into sin; yet you made us your
 covenant-partners, your agents in the earthly
 realm.
We are guardians of a tender and fragile atmosphere.
 Shifting clouds, hurricanes and blizzards, these
 are humanity's foster children.
Farmland and forests, mountains and rivers, all have
 been placed in our safekeeping; we are pastors of
 every city and town, the overseers of civilization.
Atoms and microbes you put under our protection; of
 elephants and rhinoceros did you give us custody.
"Treat my oceans with tenderness," says the Lord,
 "and guard the innocent land from plunder!"

In fear and awe we behold mystery within mystery; we
 ponder one-celled organisms, and fathom the
 velvet depths of space.
By thunder and calm your Name is praised, O Holy
 One; singing and weeping, your people encircle
 the earth with praise.
You, O God, are Sovereign of the Darkness and Ruler
 of the Light. Out of your Word the glorious,
 terrible universe came to be!

*C*rocodiles and Pandas

*O*nly to you, O God, do we offer rafter-rattling
   praise! We worship you with joyful noise and loud
   reverence!
Only to you, O Holy One, does creation belong; only
   to you do we owe our lives. Thanks be to God!
You are Divine Father and Eternal Mother; you anguish
   over the transgressions and pain of all your children.

Upon your altar, O God, we place our troubled spirits;
   at your holy table we confess:
Jealousy and harsh deceit have stained our hearts. We
   have become people who exploit the helpless.
Without hesitation we plunder creation and tyrannize
   the weak; each day we sentence the innocent to
   lives of desolation.
Only your righteousness, O Shaper of History, can
   cover our sin; your forgiveness stretches across the
   dream-webbed reaches of space.

Standing in the ungentle sun of the marketplace, we
   proclaim our repentance. No longer will we
   pledge allegiance to the fat gods of prosperity.

No longer will we participate in destroying human
   dignity; nor will we enslave ourselves to comfort
   that is purchased at the expense of another's life.
We repent ourselves of power that bargains in cruelty;
   we reject all vicious and slanderous speech.
Our public announcement is this: We will not auction
   our heritage for gold and silver; nor will we accept
   military strength in the place of Yahweh's
   salvation-promise.

A ransomed and forgiven people, we are released for
   hope! You, O God, have brought us out of
   degradation into glory!
You keep watch through the night with those who
   grieve; you deliver the sin-ridden from their
   torment.
It is not in your nature, O Sustainer of All, to forsake
   your people. You will never abandon us to the
   immoderate appetites of evil.

Out of nothing you created ringed planets and thick
   moons. As a child scatters a handful of jacks, you
   dispersed galaxies across the rich, calm darkness.
You built up the mountain ranges and seeded the vine-
   tangled forests; from the morning mist you called
   forth monkeys and crocodiles and pandas.
Wisdom created the airless, blue-cold mass of glaciers;
   your hand shaped icy worlds that echo with the
   sounds of winters past.
With earth and sky as midwife, Yahweh birthed new
   possibility into being: And the divine birth pangs
   issued forth in humankind.

Walking in the hallowed paths of our ancestors, we
    bear witness to the staggering power and
    boundless generosity of creation.
The Spirit-filled ones sense now the rejoicing of rocks
    and the soaring harmony of eagles. Blessed are
    those who perceive the reflection of Ultimate
    Energy in a silent smile.
You are at work, O God, bending each vulnerable
    moment to your unearthly purpose. You demolish
    the gray walls that separate creation from itself.
In this historical moment, O Holy One, you are
    tearing down the barbed wire erected by sin.
    Incarnate Destiny is overturning the rule of death.

Let us dedicate ourselves to the newborn day! Let us
    celebrate the Hallelujah-morning of forgiveness!
Sing out with resolute voice: Yahweh at last has set the
    captives free!
If your voice is silent, clap your hands: Despair is
    already routed!
If you are unable to hear, stamp your feet: Steadfast
    love has vanquished death!
If your feet cannot move, feel the atoms within you
    rejoicing: All life belongs to the Life-giver!
    Thanks be to God!

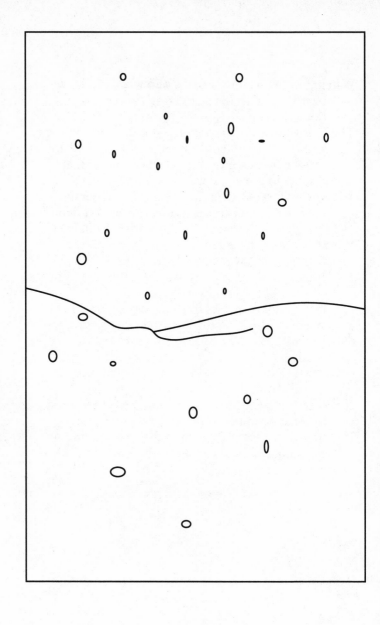

This Winter Season

*R*elieve my distress, O Lord of Life; deliver me from the treacherous, cold web of sin.

Though I am a creature without merit, though I am devoid of all righteousness, you are the God of covenant; you will not forsake me.

Remember the wild energy and awful wonder of the promise you made. Recall the immortal, resounding covenant to which you have bound yourself.

Before time ever raised its head out of the primitive bog, you declared yourself to be our God; before the beginningless beginning, you chose the creation.

In this, my winter season, do not turn away. I have mixed my imperfect clay with repentance and tears.

There is no part of me that is not polluted, defiled, crushed by the weight of sin; I am like an aged woman raving in the streets, a separated particle of humanity.

In secret did I plant bitter, impenitent falsehood, and
from my lies sprang forth a poisonous tree.
I have indentured myself to death-in-life; I am a sign
and a terror to all who behold me.
The artful gods of power and opulence have wrapped
me in their ghastly embrace; I have descended
into the molded pit of corruption.

But your compassion, O Holy One, has no beginning,
no end; every repentant cry reaches the eternal
throne.
Draw me again out of the womb; with new and
enduring letters, write my name on the face of
creation.
Transform the sad way of treachery into dawn-infused
faith, render my guilt into confidence and
courage.
Into my stricken body breathe the bright wind of God;
refresh me with your salvation-spirit.

You and you alone, O God, can turn sin inside out;
you have the power to transform wrong into
righteousness.
Once again, O Mystery, throw me onto the potter's
wheel; reshape the clay in accordance with your
triumphant, unearthly purpose.
Visit me with the strengthening power of your Spirit;
fold the ends of heaven around me like a
baptismal garment.
Dissolve the hardness of my heart and sustain me as
the river upholds a raft; my desire is to serve you

with singleness of spirit and with full-voiced
praise.

My empty hands, O Lord, you have blessed; the
threads of my shattered and broken life have been
woven into the whole cloth of humanity.
In yielding I have found welcome; in surrender,
strength.
By offering all, I have gained all; by renouncing pride,
I am cleansed of illusion.

Out of misery has sprouted possibility. You have
wrenched me from death and propelled me into
victorious life.
Surely your severe and corrective mercy, O God, is the
same as your passionate, loving judgment. Each
day and each night I will glory in your extravagant
Mystery.
Throughout this luminous, destinal journey I will tell
the good news; with every breath I will proclaim
the forever-story of sin overcome.

Beatitude

*J*oyful is she who sets her heart upon God; anxiety
     has no power over her.
To him who discovers freedom in Yahweh will be
     granted strength and serenity; day after day he
     will grow in wisdom.
Favor and blessing is lavished upon the ones who
     discern Ultimate Mystery in the fabric of creation;
     these are the pure in heart.
Evil will not prevail over him who perceives holiness in
     a grasshopper. She will flourish who beholds
     God's Spirit in a disabled child.

But those who dishonor the Almighty, those who
     divest creation of its dignity, will find themselves
     broken apart.
The cyclone of divine judgment shall visit those who
     hurl violence into the midst of innocent lives; the
     empires of those who exploit human suffering will
     be demolished.

The saints are those who adhere to God, and only
     God; their obedience gives birth to ceaseless
     vitality and an incorruptible spirit!

They are like spacewalkers, unfettered by gravity;
    weightless and free, they move through a region
    of unexplored mystery!
To them, the way of Yahweh resounds with confidence
    and awe; they celebrate the incarnation of God's
    justice.
Their joy comes from caring for the downtrodden,
    their fulfillment from reaching out to the
    heartbroken and to the weary.

Those who reject the Preserver of Life are haunted by
    murderous dreams and elusive hopes. But Yahweh
    lifts the burdens of those whose hearts and minds
    are pure.
The children of the Holy One are adorned with
    becoming; by the joyous embrace of eternal life
    they are cradled.

Absalom! Absalom!

*L*ike those who hear far-off drums, we sense the
    approach of judgment; the enduring Word echoes
    within our bones.
Yahweh cries out to a broken humanity; God
    summons the stars to bear witness against us.
There is no limit to the Redeemer's untamable love;
    the Holy One will not be dissuaded from
    dispensing mercy.

Already we have seen our illusions shattered; the skies
    have darkened and the waters run foul with
    poison.
Corruption is commonplace, and Earth is convulsed
    with violent death.
Despots are replaced by despots; fossil fuel burns like a
    sacrifice to alien gods.
But the eye of the hurricane is the eye of God; at the
    heart of the living storm is Yahweh's covenant-
    love.

Thus says the Lord our God: "I have had pity on those
    undeserving of pity; with a faithless people, I have
    kept faith.

You have cried out to me and I have answered you;
　　but your allegiance is to outward appearances.
You avoid the disheveled, shambling beggars; coins in
　　the poor box, O woman, do not acquit you of
　　wrong.
Do not think that I await your worship, O man; you
　　have made of me a hired servant.
The blessings I bestow, you accept as your due; my
　　judgment you dismiss as bad fortune.
You have become blind to the fire and the cloud; your
　　ears no longer hear the voice of the prophets.

"My people, have you forgotten that faith is not
　　certainty? Have you lost sight of the energy found
　　in desert places?
Why do you forsake the wilderness where I led you
　　from bondage into holiness? Why do you reject
　　the water that flows from the Rock of Truth?"

We are created without divisions: In the sight of the
　　Giver of Peace, we are neither male nor female,
　　neither healthy nor infirm.
God's righteousness is justice for every creature; the
　　law of Yahweh countermands hatred and strikes
　　down prejudice.
The poor and wealthy alike are judged by the Holy
　　One. "Have you loved one another?" asks the
　　Ruler of History. "And have you loved me, my
　　beloved?"

*F*rom the *Deeps*

*T*urn me around, O God of Hosts; shelter me with
your steadfast love.

Too long have I avoided your fierce, unshakable Word.
Numbing my senses day after day, I have built a
fortress of death.

Hear my stumbling, repentant cry, O God; do not
withhold your mercy from one who has run out
of hope.

I am flayed and shredded and scattered by sin; apathy
and despair cast lots for my soul.

Those close to me retreat to the sidelines; they observe
my struggle like spectators at a prizefight.

An alien horizon surrounds me; I am defined by clocks
and money.

I am lost in an unbroken line of traffic, hurrying
without destination. In the floodwaters of
progress I am drowning.

Truth is replaced by "deviations from exactitude,"
honesty by "plausible deniability."

I am strangled by endless, serpentine lies; falsehood
embalms my words.

History seems to be out of control; chemicals are ever-present in the fabric of life.

Within my own body I am a displaced person, a refugee from reality.

My soul yearns to connect with creation; I cry out for the Unconditional, for the Eternal.

I yearn for Meaning to seize me, to shake me loose from the tyranny of Earth's time.

Peace-making lies beyond my reach and beyond my power; no human being can calm the unreconciled heartbeat of society.

But you, O Holy One, stand responsible for all that is. Only your voice can silence the telephones and sirens and loudspeakers.

My testimony is this: Despair is not the final word; apathy will not blot out the human spirit,

Because at the bottom of the pit is not apathy, not hopelessness, not desolation. At the bottom of the pit is the rule of God!

Yahweh is Sovereign of the abyss, Lord of every desert place. Where time collides with eternity—there do we find Incarnate Meaning.

Our roots are in you, O Lord, and in no other; all nourishment comes from the Giver of Life.

As a father smoothes the brow of his child, you keep us in your everlasting care; you will never

abandon your people to the world's abusive
values.

You are not dismayed by human weakness, nor will
you be dissuaded from your covenant; even when
we wander like errant children, you will not turn
away.

Though we be flayed and torn apart, you will not
discard us. You will never take back your decree of
mercy.

At the bottom of the pit is not apathy, not
hopelessness, not despair. At the bottom of the pit
is the rule of God!

Ragman

*M*y soul vibrates with luxuriant hope; each sunrise I
greet with praise.

As light purges the sky of darkness, let us come
together to extol the Lord.

Proclaim with loud voice the pulsing grace of God!
With vehement colors create a mural of
thanksgiving!

Announce the good news! The afflicted are healed,
and the lost have been returned home!

Bear witness to my story, O women and men of the
covenant.

Sin separated me from all I had known; I lived in the
shadowy company of forgotten souls.

My comfort came from sidewalk grates; discarded
newspapers were my only shelter.

Out of the city's terror-depths, I cried to God. And
from the ashes of desolation, hope reignited within
me.

The Word of life loomed over my rag-wrapped
existence, and I was snatched from the grasp of
the cruel, accusatory streets.

Clarity entered the wicked darkness, and this homeless
man was saved by Ultimate Truth.

Know, my people, that every night must die; even the
glory-filled sunrise is tinged with mortality.
But those without power are the beloved of God; the
helpless are Yahweh's sacred people.
Holy bread rains upon the fearful and grief-stricken,
and healing will come to the vanquished outcast.
The world of idolaters will be turned upside down;
those who clothe themselves with privilege are
under the judgment of Yahweh.

Hear my words, O sisters and brothers: God our
Redeemer is one God.
We are the ancestors of the future; we stand on the
precipice of a holy and terrible moment.
Neither the guests, nor the victims of God, we have
been chosen into responsibility. We are the
servants and care-givers of creation.

Listen, O forgiven people: Out of Fathomless Mystery
comes salvation.
It is Yahweh who brings forth life, and Yahweh who
demands each death.
Freedom belongs to those who forsake the worship of
self; fierce-glowing hope is the inheritance of
those who seek God.
Turn to the Lord in awe and fear! Honor the One who
conceived and nurtured the heavens!

Let the frail and downtrodden arise! Let us rejoice in
the bright, humble air!
Because Yahweh will not allow hell to smother us; the
resolute love of God will not be defeated.
It is the Holy One who brings new life out of
corruption, God who rescues the afflicted and
comforts the stricken.

With overflowing praise I greet the daybreak! There is
no limit to my rejoicing!
The Giver-Destroyer has heard the bitterness of my
shriek, and Wisdom has carried me back from the
abyss.
This is the Word of God: The heavenly table has been
spread, and not one inhabitant of creation will be
turned away.
On the last day, each one will be brought home, each
one in the company of all the living who have ever
lived.
Myriad voices will infuse every corner of space, and
history will wear a crown of holy peace.

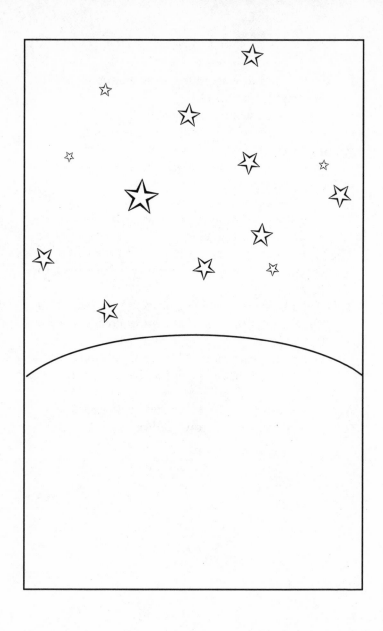

Earth and All Stars

*P*raise God with language—every dialect of earth!
Dance to honor the Holy One's covenant; play the
    world's music to worship the Lord!

Arise, all nations! We are Australia and Europe and
    Asia;
We are Mid-East and Africa, the Americas of South
    and North, telling the power of God.

Give honor to Yahweh, O parrots and pythons and
    elephants and skylarks! Tremble with holy fear,
    you dolphins and llamas and wolves and raccoons.
Let the bears of the earth and the lions rejoice; let
    bluefish and butterflies offer up praise!

Amazon and Nile, Mississippi and Danube: Every river
    professes one Origin, one Source.
From God comes the beauty and harshness of deserts:
    Sahara and Negev, Kalahari, Death Valley.
A heartbeat is pulsing from deep in the waters:
    Superior and Caspian, Atlantic and Arctic.

Everest and McKinley, Kilimanjaro and Matterhorn:
    The mountains of earth all witness to God.

To everything that is, the Holy One responds; God is
    not absent or indifferent in history.
The Lord our God is one God forever; Yahweh
    responds to both evil and good.
Like a woman protecting her endangered child, God
    shields creation with covenant-love.

From God comes the roaring destruction of avalanche;
    from Yahweh the snowmelt that waters the valley.
Of God is the soil that is teeming with summer, to the
    Holy One belongs every fruit-heavy bush,
The scuttling creatures, the unshackled hawk, the
    caverns and waterfalls and uncharted forests.

Let all the mysteries beyond earth give glory; from
    beyond the Milky Way sing out with praise!
Let galaxy clusters rejoice as they circle; let invisible
    matter praise Yahweh our God!
With quasars and dust has covenant been made; out of
    nothing, creation was shaped and set free.

In the beginning was Radical Love, twisting and
    hurling and forming creation.
On newly shaped space-time the Spirit descended;
    Yahweh gave life to the seen and unseen.
Yahweh it was who worded the universe. Laughing
    and weeping, God baptized the world.

History belongs to the Lord of creation; time and
  eternity give praise to God.
Pushed from the nest into Yahweh's freedom, all
  creatures of earth will at last be redeemed.
Come, let us follow the cloud and the fire! Come, let
  us follow the one holy star!
With every language give praise to Yahweh! With every
  dialect, glorify God!

Elijah's Mantle

Give glory to God, O people of the Promise! Keep
    ever before you the Name of Yahweh!
Fortunate are those who follow Wisdom; fulfillment
    belongs to the ones who wrestle with God.
Life abundant will be granted to the woman who lives
    the covenant; adversity will not crush her.
Happy is the man who chooses the way of passionate
    obedience; he shall witness the uprising of joy
    from the cinders of chaos.
Favored of God is the child who befriends the outcast,
    the child who shares the gift of play with those
    who have been shattered and abused.

When Truth is scourged by earthly powers, the
    righteous remain as steady as stone; neither
    threats nor coercion will shake their faith.
The righteous do not shrink from the unbearable
    anguish of a rape victim; they refuse to rob an old
    man of his gaunt dignity.
Through every barren, fear-choked night, the people
    of God keep watch; they offer hope to the
    alcoholic and to the chronically ill.

Those who proclaim Yahweh enter boldly into the presence of suffering; they bring comfort to the dying, food to the hungry, sustenance to the unemployed.

Devotion to Yahweh is alive in those who give refuge to the stranger. Virtue resides in the fierce and steadfast protection of innocent lives.

But those who deal in monopoly and control will be destroyed by their own empires; every monument to mortal glory will crumble under the judgment of God.

To withhold justice is to provoke divine wrath; none can escape Yahweh's anger toward greed and exploitation.

In the journey of faith, generosity always gives birth to joy, and trust engenders courage.

Without the Holy One we can do nothing; our efforts are as transient as wisps of fog upon a forested mountain.

It is the Giver of Life who bestows meaning, the Ruler of All who imparts grace.

O worship the Judge and Redeemer of All! Offer to God the clean, true sacrifice of unwavering justice!

Stand before Wisdom in joyous humility; show forth God's exuberant love!

To a Silent God

*T*hough I have resolved to keep silence, though I
  have promised to confide only in the walls that
  encircle my life like a boa constrictor,
Nevertheless, I must shout one final cry into the
  heedless void. The Holy One must hear the
  indictments I have prepared.

I direct my prayer to a silent God, to One who seems
  both deaf and speechless.
O Mystery above all Mystery, you watched as your
  people were exterminated; when everyday life was
  desecrated, you stood mute.
Nor was your voice heard in the aftermath of
  exploding bombs. Where was Wisdom when
  bodies were torn apart in airports and restaurants
  and schoolrooms?

I have accumulated a lifetime of outrage. My burden is
  too great for one frail creature to bear.
For decades I have wandered, an unwelcome sojourner
  dependent on the charity of others; I am a poor
  woman, driven by horrors witnessed and relived.

And now they have judged me insane; I am
	condemned to wander an endless corridor
	inhabited by the living dead.

Though I am exhausted from the burden of memory,
	and life holds no promise, I am determined to
	survive.
One must survive who will not allow God to forget;
	one must endure to enumerate the transgressions
	of the Lord.
I recall adults and children being loaded onto trucks;
	they were shot by human predators and their
	bodies buried in empty gold mines.
My eyes have witnessed soldiers firing into a crowd of
	students; arms linked, they died with incredulous
	looks forever captured on their faces.
I keep before me the names of those held hostage;
	pawns in a twisted, violent game, they live at the
	mercy of baleful, wild-eyed men.

The world is built on bones crying out to be
	unearthed, bones waiting to be breathed into
	fulfillment by the Word of God.
We are the dead who are living and the living who are
	dead; we wait for your universal voice, O God, to
	penetrate the murderous din of hell.
Rise up and defend yourself, O Lord. You are the
	Giver of Peace, and yet peace is as short-lived as a
	snowflake that lands on an outstretched palm.

Why are the innocent judged along with the guilty?
   Must children grow up with the stench of atrocity
   in their nostrils?
Are you punishing all for the sins of some? Have you
   abandoned humanity to inevitable, bitter suicide?

Hear my bitter, intransigent complaint, O God; do not
   let your enemies triumph; they have planted the
   flag of madness on your once-innocent creation.
You are Sovereign of All; your hand can save us, your
   redemption can heal even the deepest scars.

Each day I contemplate the bars across my window; I
   am a captive of the State, a disgraceful exception
   to society's order.
They have judged me insane so that no one will listen
   to my rambling speech, so that no one will read
   the impolite anguish of my words.
I am housed in a tower of iniquity; my body is
   convulsed by mourning for my own death.
Before long these bones will be discarded; they will be
   thrown upon the world's stockpile of forgotten
   lives.
How long can I stay alive, O God? How long before
   my life ends, strangled by a rope of desperation?

Emmanuel

God is my protector and defender; Yahweh watches over my battered, sleeping body.

Only God knows my real name, the one I whisper to myself when I hide in the stairwell.

When I escape from the father who is hard-faced and threatful, Yahweh is my steadfast companion.

The Holy One stands guard while I wait in an alcove, pressed motionless against the sullen plaster walls.

When I am pursued by the gangs, it is Yahweh who guides me; God is my safe-passage through the intricate maze of violence.

There is no pain that God does not feel, no blow that does not strike the Giver of Life.

From the Ruler of History, I have learned hope. I have learned by heart the story of God's steadfast love for a people in bondage.

From you, O Wisdom, come the ones who do not punish, the courageous ones who resist the onrush of evil.

Sometimes, in a quiet classroom, I dream about freedom; far from the roar of poverty, I feel the breath of God upon me.

My fear scatters like summer dust when the woman
who lives next door begins to sing. With music
floating lonesome and strong across the
fire escapes, my spirit at last rejoices.

Not a rock moves but that you see it, O God; no
creature cries out alone.
Through the labyrinth of forsaken streets, the Holy
One travels with me; there is no place too terrible
for Yahweh to enter.
You are my defender and protector, O Holy One; you
are my shield against the poisonous mix of love
and hate.
With your Word to strengthen me, I will flee the
devouring sewers; I will not perish in the streets,
Because your Name is Everlasting. You are the
safekeeper of creation: You challenge every
injustice; you watch through every ravaging night.

Safe House

*T*he traveler-with-God will find asylum; Yahweh's
    mothering wings will shelter him who chooses the
    fearsome way of trust.
With spiritual waters, bitter and sweet, will Yahweh
    refresh the traveler.

When you are lost, Yahweh will find you; like a parent
    whose child has disappeared, God will search.
When the corrupt of the earth utter their threats
    against you, God's unshakable Word thunders
    across the night.
"I am not mocked," says the Lord; "nor shall my
    people be humiliated."
When moneylenders take away your life, or when
    addiction ensnares you, then will God shatter the
    chains; then will Yahweh's wrath splinter the
    captors' power.
Though the oppressors hide behind their wealth,
    though they flee from prosecution, they cannot,
    they will not, escape God's righteous and holy
    wrath.

Know that God is for you: Yahweh, the Judge and the
    Advocate of Creation.

And because God is for you, you will not be consumed
    by the world's fetid chaos.
Though violence and fear cleave the urban night, you
    will not be daunted; despair will not write your
    name in the book of the living dead.
Though governments silence your voice, Yahweh will
    send messengers to guide you; they will lead you
    across the mountains into a new land, a land of
    freedom and hope.
Though you be paralyzed by anxiety and smothered by
    grief, God's healing Word will wrest you from the
    edge of the pit.

Thus says the Lord: "The woman who trusts in me
    will see Ultimate Truth; she who takes refuge in
    obedience will be comforted.
No one seeking the shelter of my Wisdom will be
    turned away; I am the First and the Last, the
    Defender and Protector of all.
I have seen creation under seige; I have seen humanity
    scattered like broken glass. But the covenant I
    made with your forebears I will not abandon."

"At the moment you were drawn from the womb,"
    says the Holy One, "I bore witness and claimed
    you as my own.
Every tear will I wipe away, every pain assuage.
And your suffering-rejoicing body I will forever clothe
    in the rainbow-garment of redemption."

In Mercy Broken

*T*he proud trust only in their own power; they seek
    not the Wisdom of God;
Covetous and boastful, they build shrines to safe,
    manageable gods. They darken their windows
    against the sight of the hungry and homeless.
Without hesitation, the arrogant ones distort truth;
    they encourage the fears and suspicions that
    destroy human kindness.
Poverty does not trouble those who worship
    competition; they bury human need under endless
    paperwork.
Some there are who isolate themselves in
    condominiums and chalets and summer homes;
    they recoil from society's tears.
Surrounded by bodyguards, the powerful ones travel
    only the known roads; each moment they stand
    ready to deny God.

Where God is not honored, humankind stumbles; we
    sink deeper and deeper into the quicksand of sin.
None can escape the snares of evil; all have fallen short
    of the glory of God.

But Yahweh knows the heart of every creature, and
Yahweh anguishes over the pain of each life.
On our hearts the Holy One has written a living law, a
law that welcomes the outcast and values the
stranger.

Dread will infuse the lives of the proud; anxiety will
confound the aggressors.
But those who embrace one another's pain, those who
weep for God and for the world, they shall sense
the victory of Infinite Mystery.
Those who hunger for justice and thirst for
compassion shall be sustained; those who seek
reconciliation will be welcomed into a radiant
fellowship.

Yahweh reigns! And the ever-dawning sky reflects
God's holy promise!
All life comes under God's governance; not one
particle of matter will ever be forsaken.
The Holy One has made a nonnegotiable pledge, a
bond that outlives suffering and temptation and
death.
With the entire created order Yahweh has made
covenant, and by this unbreakable covenant we
are guarded and guided, shielded and challenged!
World without end! Amen.

The Trial

Before the powers of the age, I stand resourceless; I
am a root growing in hell.

My enemies have set for me a trap of deceit; in the
deadly chill of a marble courtroom, they fabricate
testimony.
Every day their briefcases click open and shut; my
enemies wear costly suits befitting a funeral.
Watching them dismantle my dreams, I am
mesmerized by the stench of ruin; before me the
lawyers pace like caged animals.
It is as though I have been caught in the undertow of
evil; my friends feed on contempt; like lifeless
bones they molder and grow hard.

But you, O God, will wipe the death-sweat from me.
You will not allow the corrupt monster to hurl me
against violent rocks.
As I make my way through dark and dangerous
tunnels, you are the lamp that goes ever before
me.

There are those who are angered by creation's
　　outrageous holiness. To them I will testify of your
　　indelible power, O God.
I proclaim that no courtroom can ever contain the
　　Uncontainable Mystery; no legal proceeding can
　　control the One who prowls the wilderness and
　　who shepherds the constellations.
Because God has chosen to speak through visionaries
　　and prophets, I will not be defeated. The
　　downtrodden and the falsely accused are
　　messengers of God's righteous Word!

Enliven me, O Holy One, to withstand the empire-
　　builders; deliver me from the shackles of their
　　perjury.
Let the truth stand lonely and clean-washed, reflecting
　　the bright light of eternity.
The future, O Lord, belongs to you, the Lover of
　　Justice, the Liberator of Captives.
Carry us forward into your kingdom! Establish your
　　realm in the midst of your broken people!

On the Edge

*I*f God is for us, who can be against us? Who shall
   defeat us when Yahweh is our God?
Though complexity bears down like an avalanche,
   though the world claims we cannot change the
   world,
Though we are paralyzed by indebtedness, though the
   planet is bathed in poison,
We shall not concede to the forces of evil! The victory
   does not belong to Satan!

Into ordinary clay Yahweh breathes life eternal. And
   God's promise is this:
The powerless will be raised up, the abused ones shall
   be comforted;
We who are rejected have already been accepted; we
   are God's glory-children, inheritors of the
   kingdom.
"Have no fear," Yahweh says. "Put aside your fear and
   be ready for action!
Be faithful, for you are living on the edge of eternity!"

God will not jettison this blue-green planet; we have
   not been abandoned to spin out of control;

Creation trembles on the brink of a wild, invisible
    future; the expanding universe takes daily
    sustenance from covenant-love.

Though progress seems about to destroy us, though
    bureaucrats manage our every decision,
Though corporations make jobs obsolete, though
    crime imprisons us in our homes,
Yahweh's limitless, enduring love will not fail! God's
    covenant will sustain us through every bone-
    crushing crisis.
Even now the Holy One is caring for the uncared for;
    in this very instant, the weak are being made
    strong.
"Be faithful!" God says. "Take on the armor of faith
    and reject the idols of wealth and prestige!
Each day and each hour, you are standing on the verge
    of victory! Already my realm is breaking
    through!"

Come together, all people! Come, let us live in
    expectation and faith!
Seize the moment from Satan. In the midst of the
    raucous marketplace, seek Yahweh's peace.
When the world calls out to us, let us break ranks and
    shout praise to the Infinite Other.
In this holy pilgrimage, we are the agents of Yahweh;
    every human decision is blessed with meaning.

If God is for us, none can be against us. None shall
    defeat us, because Yahweh is Sovereign.

We shall not concede to the forces of evil! The victory
    does not belong to Satan!
Thus says the Lord: "I have planted you on my holy
    mountain; each day I provide you with holy food!
Your treasure is a spiritual treasure; your wealth can
    neither be stolen nor lost!
You are living on the edge of eternity! On the verge of
    final victory do you stand!"

*E*nter the River

*C*onsider the wholeness that flows from God!
Behold the unbounded salvation that Yahweh
bestows!

Hear my witness, born of desolate wandering; listen to
the Word that was revealed when the universe
shifted.
With practiced cunning, the world caught me in its
furious embrace; the hollow ones drew me into
fatal currents of deceit.
Like a worm burrowing in the earth, I searched out
information; I traded in stolen words.
Success was my god, and wealth my destination, until
God's shattering event uncovered my secret
treachery.

Yahweh alone is the Source of Truth; no other can
redeem us from hell's torrential energy.
To the Holy One give your allegiance; reject the
devouring gods of competition.
Do not deify achievement, nor worship at the
crumbling altar of self-sufficiency.

What lies beyond today is not progress, not the distant
horizon of human perfection; what sustains today
and beyond today is the healing power of God.

Value every particle of creation; bind yourself to the
audacious flow of holy history.
Surrender to God, and from the world's tenebrous
power you will be freed; a soaring crescendo of
possibility will replace the emptiness within.
Do not allow the powerful to extort from you their
measure of pride; they will blackmail you with
your own greed.
Choose instead for the Holy One; like a spacewalker,
step out with courage into God's unencumbered
future.

Faith relinquishes earthly support, faith trusts wholly
in God; and the fruit of trust is unshakable
serenity.
Join with me in loud rejoicing! We are no longer
imprisoned by sin!
Yahweh has removed the tarnish of every past; an
abundance of grace is our true inheritance.
Let us arise and enter the River of Being! Come with
me and claim the resplendent freedom of God!

*L*ion of Judah

*F*rom the depths of mortal being I offer praise! I
glorify God with every breathing shred of energy!
It is Yahweh who confers peace upon the anguished
heart, the Enabler of Life who rekindles the
apathetic spirit.
To God belongs all healing, all wholeness; the Holy
One nurses creation with the milk of redemption.
We are a rag-tag, remnant people; only in Yahweh's
covenant-goodness does our destiny lie.

Our faith is in the one God, the Creator of all that is
seen and of all that cannot be seen.
Through the awesome unfolding of time we see God
at work revealing God; Wisdom permeates the
fragile membrane of history.

Those with inner eyes, bear witness to the victory of
divine love! Those with true ears, listen to the
continuing beat of life!
Creator-love embraces the imperfect ones; broken and
doubting and believing, the saints travel onward
in refulgent hope.

The ways of Yahweh are not our ways; we cannot
fathom the Unfathomable One.
Yahweh shatters human expectation; the Holy One
liberates us with the shocking, comforting Word
of repentance.
When we are certain of judgment, we are surprised
by forgiveness. In the midst of death, hope
springs forth like living water.
Eternal life has no price, nor can Yahweh's steadfast
love be earned.
The Source of All is free without limit; in perfect
freedom God judges and forgives and redeems.
Yahweh is Totally Other, Mystery above mystery, and
God is also Intimate Companion, the partner of
fallible creation.

Glorify God, you prophets and martyrs: you who
make of your lives a living witness!
Give honor to Yahweh, you teachers and healers: you
who do battle with pain and illusion!
Worship the Lord, you preachers and children: you
who challenge injustice and wrong!

Do not be deafened by the mechanical clamor of
human power; listen always for the Lion's
unearthly roar.
Watch for the beacon of Truth; stay alert for the
ingressing of salvation!

From the astonished center of myself, I give thanks to God! As one who has been rescued and restored, I offer unceasing praise to the Holy One!

Hands

*T*o you I offer all honor and praise, O Infinite
    Mystery; affliction has not subdued me, nor has
    despair destroyed my soul.
When my ears lost all strength and hearing perished,
    you, O God, did not desert me.
When I raged against the unyielding approach of
    silence, you heard my complaint.
When the spoken word became a sour tormented
    memory, you rescued me.

O people of God, let us rehearse together the holy
    story.
Shape words with your hands, so that my eyes might
    read them.
Stamp with your feet, so that my body might feel the
    vibration of praise.
Dance out the story of Yahweh's freedom; pound like
    the storm that crushes injustice and protects the
    afflicted.

My story is this: In former days I reveled in the world's
    trivial uproar. Proud and aloof, I forged new
    images of self-conceit.

And then, rounding a sudden corner, I collided with
the limits of human knowing.
Like the brooding tide, sound receded from me; I
could not even hear myself when I cursed the
indifferent universe.
Under the weight of Divine Mystery, faith crumbled;
thick clouds closed around my soul.
Human speech inverted; it crumbled like the barren
relic of another time.
Life, for me, upended; it seemed as though I had
plunged into the cold, seamless river of space.

With scientific care I recorded the transgressions of the
Almighty; I computed the sum of divine injustice.
No comfort would I seek; I remained in narrow,
dream-ridden exile, weaving a tapestry of God's
wrongdoing.

But you, O Creator of Mystery, descended into the
stern oblivion of hell; with holy oil you anointed
my unfaith.
To me you sent a human messenger, an angel who
offered the blessing of a new language.
Her hands created speech; once again, words animated
my narrow and scornful world.
Silence was enlivened by hope; rock-hard reality
shifted to reveal unbounded possibility.
And beyond the stillness, beyond terror, I sensed the
breathing of Almighty God.

For ever and ever I will make known your mercy, O
Lord of Life. Death will not prevent me, nor will
terror defeat my praise.
Sorrow has finally lost its wild, ashen power; to you, O
God, I offer an excess of joy.
For ever and ever I will shape lavish hymns of clean-
burning faith; my hands will create limitless songs
of thanksgiving!

The Other Side

*L*iving in the midst of a broken and decaying world,
    I am God's witness. My heart has been turned
    and returned; my spirit is released within me.
In the presence of all God's children, I shout; I sing
    with joy: The Holy One will never forsake the
    faithful!

In former times, envy corrupted my heart; then it was
    that I lost faith with holy history.
The community of the covenant I rejected, and I
    discarded my heritage. Wandering from place to
    place, I collected evidence against the sovereignty
    of God.

Everywhere around me, the corrupt ones enjoyed the
    best of fortunes; prosperity embraced the dishonest.
With the eyes of my obsession I viewed a world built
    on injustice; I saw a social order that rewards the
    cynical and welcomes the arrogant.
Those who deny the Holy One are well-fed and well-
    clothed; their sleep is untroubled.

The worshipers of fame all laugh at my sacrifice; they
   live in opulence and splendor at the expense of
   the poor.
Those who lay off workers and shut down factories
   feast at sumptuous tables. They walk quickly past
   the women and men who huddle in doorways.
When the homeless ones encroach upon their lives,
   business owners vote to put rat poison in the
   garbage cans, in the places where discarded food
   is sought by the poor.
Industrialists dump toxic waste by night, and by day
   they hide behind denials. They treat the world as
   if it were a replaceable machine.
Politicians avert their eyes from dying and hungry
   children; they argue that malnutrition is
   inevitable.
With suggested threats and legal blackmail, our leaders
   manipulate the future. They have created a system
   of evil, a web of selfishness and cruelty.

Competition, not compassion, drives the earth-bound
   forward; without question, they have given up on
   humanity.
Their dream is for themselves alone; they set
   themselves above God and above Mystery-born
   creation.
Homage is paid to the wealthy and famous; these are
   established as worthy models for the new
   generation.

Everywhere Yahweh is mocked; the faithless dismiss
God as but another human creation, they declare
faith to be a relic of the past.

Yes, there was a time when the cynical, jaded ones
ensnared me; I doubted then that Wisdom had
spoken the whole truth.

My spirit became uneasy, and I yearned to take the
wide and the smooth path. I surrounded myself
with material goods and also with carnal
pleasures.

Practicality seemed more valid than obedience; I
despaired of following the One who is shrouded
in Mystery.

To God I insisted: The world's comforts are mine by
right! I am not Hosea or Jeremiah; it is not my
task to speak on behalf of the suffering ones!

Then, in the midst of that outcry, the anguish of
Yahweh broke through; the Exodus God
shattered the illusion, and my blinders were torn
off!

God's reality pierced my delusions; in the face of a
poverty-ravaged woman I saw the reflection of my
own life.

On the other side of numbness, I repented; I rejected
the blind words of self-indulgence.

Those who believe they can shape the universe or
     design destiny will not stand! Their spirits will be
     eroded by hopelessness and doubt.
Having everything to lose, they fear loss like a hunted
     animal fears the predatory beast.
Those who pledge allegiance to competition have
     indentured themselves to death; their world is
     already crumbling, but they cannot see it.
When adversity sweeps from them their luxurious
     homes, they will drown in the undertow; they
     cannot survive.
When mortality claims a beloved child, or when
     disease erases a dream, self-determination does
     not suffice.

I confess that I turned away from the faith of my
     mothers; I rejected the obedient trust of my
     fathers.
My soul languished in self-pity; I ignored the
     testimony of the prophets and the good news of
     the saints.
I was seduced, but now I am healed; I was isolated,
     but now I am restored.
Mine is not a solitary journey; I take my place with all
     the living who have ever lived and with all the
     living who are yet to be.
I am the forebear of God's future; in my safekeeping
     has been placed the holy-glory tradition of the
     One who rides in the desert.

When the hope beyond hope appears, when we sense
the passing-by of God, then the world's mortal
power trembles!
Our hope is well-founded; it rests in a profound
awareness of holy destiny, and in the perception
that nothing at all has power apart from Yahweh.
We who hope in the Lord of Life will never give up:
We will never give up on one another, and we will
never give up on those who have given up on
themselves.
Neither the down-and-out, nor the apathetic, nor the
despairing ones will ever be turned away, because
everything that is, belongs to the Lord of Hosts.
Humanity is neither the victim, nor the guest of God;
all of us are covenant-partners with Yahweh; we
are colleagues with God in an eternal, cosmic
carnival of joy and light and ultimate good!

Maelstrom

O Judge of All Things, deliver your servant; do not
  decline to hear my case.
The world has buckled and warped beneath me;
  nothing remains except to confess.
I have heard the voice of the prophet; out of the
  wilderness comes his cry:
"Repent of your stubbornness, reunite with your God;
  be cleansed in the river of steadfast love!"

From my body the flesh has melted; my voice rasps
  like an ancient woman's.
With slow agony do I form each word; like rain
  eroding a hillside, addiction has stolen my
  lifeblood.
Aloud I mourn for the person I once was, for the
  person I no longer see in the mirror.
Restlessness invades my waking hours; violent dreams
  inhabit the night.
Even now the demons hold fast; I cannot shake loose
  of their murderous grasp.

Brutal craving has robbed my children of food; I fear
  that no job can hold me, no human words reach
  my inner core.

Too many times have I chased down alleyways; too
often have I visited the house of the Evil One.
Every reminder—every rock, every pipe—drives me
back; jeering, the suppliers await my return.
The image of death continues to beckon; I am a guest
of the courts of darkness.
Abandoned by those I once called friends, I am
drowning in limitless shame; all have fled as
though they had seen a rotting corpse.

Only to you, O Holy One, can I confess my sin; only
your majesty is more powerful than death.
No longer can I remain in hiding; every detail of my
obsession have I revealed.
Though disease impairs my understanding, though the
drugs still claim me as their own, I will not
surrender.
Too long have I endured alone; I am crushed by the
weight of unconfessed sin.
No disease is beyond your healing, O God; everything
draws sustenance from your abundant grace.

You heard my plea, O Lord, and embraced my pain;
your forgiveness has pried open the doors of hell.
Your human messengers visited me, you sent
comforters to speak the Word of hope;
And so, when night sweats and tremors threaten me, I
am not dismayed; by the counsel of angels I am
strengthened to do battle each day.

My heart is set upon you and you alone, O God; mine
is the discipline of trust and the path of daily
courage.
Because you have paid the ransom, terror no longer
owns me; possibility accompanies each breath.
With exploding life you shattered the demons' power;
despair has been turned inside out.

Great and victorious is the Holy One! This fragile life
has been given a second chance!
Rejoice, all peoples! From even the drug houses our
Lord is not absent.
Ultimate power belongs to Yahweh; God has
dominion over infinite space.
Nothing can break the covenant: not addiction, nor
degradation, nor even death itself.
By extravagant love I have been rescued; sing of the
triumph and power of God!

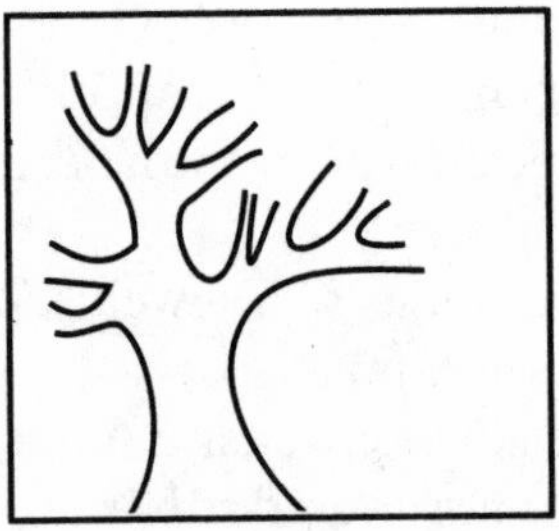

Skywalker

*L*ift every voice and sing! Sing out with heart and
    hands and voices!
Gather the people of every nation, so that all the world
    might give thanks to God!

The graciousness of Yahweh knows no limit; the
    Source of Holiness is at work in the shadows and
    alive in the places of light.
God befriends the orphan who wanders an alien land;
    the Redeemer explodes across history in order to
    free a nation in bondage.
Know that, in God, the humble are exalted and the
    bereaved find comfort. With those who have
    single-hearted trust does Yahweh keep watch.
Do not fear when your body is hungry or your spirit is
    thirsty; the Holy One provides enough for each
    day.

Before beginnings, Yahweh began; and the
    Unsearchable Word declared *all* into being.
Every creature was blessed, and each was given a
    name.

95

We are sojourners, we are pilgrims and seekers: fragile
creatures traveling through cosmic space.

Present yourselves now before God who is Mother and
Father; let creation embrace the untainted peace
of God.
Faithful and reliable is the Holy One, God who is
present wherever needed; God who is abounding
in grace and steadfast in love.
By the standard of justice is the world judged; all are
measured against the canon of love.
In the Holy One there is no barrier between male and
female, no distinction between rich and poor.
Happy are they who seek God in the eyes of every
living creature.

Everything that is, belongs to God! Because we are
citizens of the kingdom, no other can claim us.
Do not look elsewhere for certainty; shun the gods of
power and competition!
Only in Yahweh will we find true peace, only in God
will we reach fulfillment.
Lift every voice and sing! Sing out with heart and
hands and voices!
Gather the people of every nation, so that all the world
might give thanks to God!

Lynch Mob

*B*ut for God, we would have been lost! Without
    Yahweh, evil would have smothered us!
When our neighbors were transformed into a bitter
    mob, you, O Lord, stepped out of the shadows.
Though they hid their faces from us, their mean and
    narrow spirits could not be concealed.
Their fear was palpable as blood; we could not stand
    against their fury.
When we were surrounded by death, when our hope
    blurred, you sent your angels into the momentum
    of hate.
Your holy, human messengers confronted the loud
    outrage; they scattered the thick cloud of savagery
    as though dismantling a bomb.

Like a firefighter who saves a child from a building in
    collapse, Infinite Mystery has rescued us.
Like one who pulls a drowning person to shore,
    Yahweh our God has carried us out of our
    affliction.
God is for us! And because God is for us, nothing
    mortal can claim victory over our spirits.

No hate group, no political system, no corrupt society
can enslave us. Ritualized terrorism will not take
us hostage in our own land.
Yahweh will never hand us over to hell; God annuls
the specious claims of death.

All creation belongs to God, our Protector and
Defender.
And God will never give us up, our Peacemaker and
Sustainer,
Because God is for us: the Source of All Questions and
the Ultimate Answer.
We worship the One who is bound by covenant; we
follow the One who carries us into a realm of
glorious possibility.

The No-People

O Giver of Life, deliver me from those who have
   stolen my birthright.
Save me, O God, from the thin, cool air of bank
   buildings, from the biscuit-colored faces of
   mortgage holders.

They have robbed me of the land that my forebears
   tilled with suffering, the earth they sowed with
   blood.
During exuberant seasons, the bankers came, their eyes
   exact and bright, and around me they wrapped
   the winding sheet of debt.
When, year after year, seedlings strangled in the dry,
   purged earth, they were the ones who watched
   from a distance like indolent birds of prey.

Plowing under the last, withered crop, I cried: O God,
   have you forgotten your servant?
Have you forsaken your covenant with creation? Surely
   the God of Ruth and the God of Joseph will not
   allow these pale, silent bankers to prevail.

And yet, each day cuts dreadful furrows into my life;
   the sun has descended to hell.

Every scrap of earth has been repossessed; nothing
    remains for the poor of the land.
I inhabit a land of doubts and shadows; by night my
    family sleeps in the skeleton of a secondhand car.
We are the no-people of a hard and godless city;
    everyone tells us to go away from this place.
    "Keep your stink and your hungry children away,"
    they shout.

But you, O God, discern every human deception; you
    know all the corrupt secrets that are hidden
    within steel-and-glass towers.
You are the Power above power; the demons of
    financial management cannot triumph.
I will trust in the breathing whirlwind of God,
    Yahweh's storm that rises to shatter the arrogant
    empires.

Reveal, O Holy One, the decay that lies behind locked
    and polished doors; unseat the ones who divide
    and unite with fragrant, delusive speech.
Do not withhold your wrath from the worshipers of
    privilege and license; roll open the tomb wherein
    the broken ones are imprisoned.
Awaken those who have become numb to the edgeless
    ache of human need; reveal the scandalous apathy
    of governments.

Each day cuts dreadful furrows into my life; the sun
    has descended to hell.

Every scrap of earth has been repossessed; nothing
    remains for the poor of the land.
I am but specks of dust, scattered across tragic streets,
    gathered into endless gutters.
Passersby turn aside and curse me; they are like corpses
    waiting for time itself to explode.

Yet in the midst of degradation, I will not succumb;
    my soul will not allow misery to become envy, or
    envy to become the cancerous worship of wealth.
When, distracted and restless, my children cling to my
    knees, I will speak of bread in the wilderness.
My daughters and sons will hear me tell of a fierce and
    powerful God, of Yahweh who heals those who
    are broken and lifts up the forsaken ones.
Though we have wandered far, and though we may
    not again see the dark, burgeoning earth,
You, O God, will carry us back to the land of promise;
    you will restore to us our birthright.

*S*haken from the Dead

*H*allelujah! Yahweh be praised!
With mind, body, and spirit I give honor to God; I
    declare the grandeur of the Almighty with every
    triumphant shout!
To the Holy One I dedicate each hour; my days are
    resonant with prayer.

Hear these words, my people: Turn away from the
    gods fashioned by humanity. Do not surrender to
    the merchandisers of false dreams.
They entice you with comfortable promises, but their
    words crumble into dust; their claims are like the
    final cries of a trapped animal.

Only One is worthy of trust, and that is Yahweh; no
    human pledge can supplant God's covenant.
Adopting earthly values is like embracing a decayed
    corpse; material possessions will never bring
    peace.
Blessed are they who have set their hearts upon God,
    the Advocate of the Powerless, the Lover of
    Justice.

Yahweh is the One who feeds us; with spiritual food
and spiritual drink are we nourished.

God opens our ears to the groans of a hurting world;
from the Holy One comes a vision born of
wilderness freedom.
Happy are they who live in faithful expectancy; in their
bones they sense the trembling of creation.
Even now the Spirit is effecting a cosmic newness; like
a gathering storm, the realm of God draws near.

Yahweh frees the hostages and reclaims the refugees;
God takes the part of the hungry and the
unemployed.
Those evicted by bureaucratic systems no longer must
live in the shadows; the Holy One brings the
exiles home.
It is Yahweh who bears the anguish of the outcast;
God will not forget the fragile ones scattered
across the earth.
With everyone who mourns does the Lord keep vigil;
each terrible darkness is dissolved by covenant
love.
God comforts the sick and provides shelter for the
homeless; to victims of human outrage Wisdom
speaks the Word of redemption.
Like an eagle fluttering over her young, Yahweh
hovers above tenement houses; God's special
protection belongs to children who have been
robbed of hope.

The Giver of Peace overturns worldly values; the Holy
    One breaks the death-grip of exploiters and
    tyrants.
In the face of Ultimate Mystery we shout Hallelujah!
    To us has been given God's way of faith and risk
    and alert obedience.
The approach of Sovereign God is almost audible!
    Divine Justice is palpable in the expectant air!
Even now the Spirit is effecting a cosmic newness; like
    a gathering storm the realm of God draws near.

Creatures of Heaven and Earth

*I*n wonder, in gratitude we present ourselves; we
   come before the Ruler of everything that is, the
   Judge of all creation.
It is Yahweh who gives us safe haven; with tender
   patience does Wisdom instruct us.
Yahweh it is who has wrested us from the depths of
   hell; our hope rides upon the rolling power of
   God.

To the Holy One who is our eternal Mother and
   never-failing Father,
   We offer all that we have and all that we are.
To the Word whose mercy shatters every illusion,
   We offer all that we have and all that we are.
To the Sustainer who transforms degradation into
   glory,
   We offer all that we have and all that we are.

To the one God from whose womb emerged the
   infinite universe of terror and beauty,
   We offer all that we have and all that we are.

To the Creator who wove galaxies and started them on
    their numinous journeys,
  We offer all that we have and all that we are.
To the Lord of history, who works through imperfect
    actions of imperfect creatures,
  We offer all that we have and all that we are.

O God, whose faithfulness will never be deterred by
    our lack of faith,
  With the silent speech of our hands we give you
    thanks.
O Giver-Destroyer, who rescues us again and again
    from self-destruction,
  With the silent speech of our hands we give you
    thanks.
O Mysterious One, who bestows perpetual wonder
    upon those we call mentally limited,
  With the silent speech of our hands we give you
    thanks.

You are the God who broke bread so that all might be
    nourished.
  With the silent speech of our hands we give you
    thanks.
You are the Suffering One who embraced finitude and
    brokenness so that all might know life.
  With the silent speech of our hands we give you
    thanks.
You are the One who exploded the power of death so
    that none who is living should ever die.

With the silent speech of our hands we give you
thanks.

Light our path across the wilderness, O God; from you
and you alone does salvation come.
World without end. Amen.
Fold us in the holy embrace of covenant-love; protect
us with your gracious and terrible mercy.
World without end. Amen.
In wonder, in gratitude we present ourselves before
you, the Origin and Aim of Life.
World without end. Amen.

Prisoner

I offer my complaint to God; with vehement words
and inarticulate moaning, I lament.
Of no crime am I guilty, and yet I wear a garment cut
from the cloth of bitter imprisonment.
I wrap myself in the thin blanket of endurance;
affliction has become my daily companion.
Strands of gray hair mingle with dark; each week more
teeth loosen in my mouth.
The demons of despair trample and desecrate my sleep;
each day my lifeblood flows down corroded
prison drains.

Prayer has not brought justice; petition has not thrown
open the clashing metal doors.
I am a creature who must live apart from sunlight; I
am robbed of the clear, free air.
Into infinite darkness my pleas reach out, stretching
until at last they snap and disintegrate.
The well-fed, comfortable ones have never known the
rank chill of a prison cell; they have replaced
God's righteousness with self-serving arguments.

Though death may claim me this very night, I cannot
   give up; I will not disclose the hiding place of my
   abused and terrified children.

In the untimely, disjointed darkness I confront the
   Giver of All Things: Is creation no longer the
   adopted child of Yahweh?
Where is the One who liberated our forebears from
   bondage to an alien nation? Have we been
   rejected and abandoned by the Holy One?
Has Yahweh's covenant-love receded like floodwaters?
   Will the Ruler of History deliver the innocent into
   the hands of the corrupt?

O God, I will not allow you to forget your eggshell-
   tender creatures. While there is life-strength
   within me, I will invoke the memory of your
   mighty actions:
The unrestrained thundering of divine judgment, and
   the palpable, rushing presence of your Holy
   Spirit.
You have declared yourself bound, O Lord of History,
   bound by one indivisible covenant;
You cannot release us from your rainbow-promise, and
   we will never be exempted from your law.

Bear witness, my people: When brand-new creatures
   are discovered in a shadowless ocean, science pays
   homage to the exuberance of Holy Mystery.

112

Constellations blaze with thanksgiving when a patient
    is released from coma, and when the despairing
    say no to suicide.
When children cross the border into the dawn-light of
    freedom, the Evil One lurches as though dealt a
    mortal blow.
It is Yahweh who causes myriad stars to form and
    reform, explode and condense, Yahweh who is
    moving toward a single, universal destiny.
Your solidarity, O God, is with the oppressed and
    abused; those without hope will someday know
    the honey-sweet taste of your blessing.

This is the night of our Passover, O God; the night on
    which we are delivered from evil and malice and
    death.
Sojourners in holy history, we follow Yahweh's Word;
    through this perilous, yet merciful wilderness the
    fire of Truth goes before us.
Accept my sacrifice of fear and faith, Redeemer-God;
    restore my exhausted spirit and renew this
    decaying body.
From this prison cell I will once again sing of salvation:
    I will tell of the onrush of grace, of healing that
    can never be thwarted!

Manna

*D*eliver us, O Sustainer of life, Protector of all that is
and all that will be.

You are Sovereign over the evening winds; each season
is birthed from the womb of God.

Your realm encompasses shivering Earth and the
fantastic, unbroken expanse of space;

Divine glory clings to every silent and lonely fragment
of matter.

Rescue us, Redeemer God, from solemn captivity.
Free us from the devouring, seductive beast of illusion.

Remember, O Holy One, how once you stalked the
earth, overturning the tables of injustice.

You shattered slaveholders, and tore your people free
from bondage to an opulent, ravenous land.

Into the wasteland—wild, alarming, and rock-
infested—you led them; you nurtured our fathers
and mothers with the humility of desert places.

You annealed them by hardship, tested them in the
crucible of suffering.

But when our forebears mourned with loud and
    terrible cries, when they proffered their sad,
    barren hands, you relented, feeding them as a
    mother feeds her newborn.

The bread of the wilderness they called "What is it?"
    Manna was the name they gave to the Exodus
    food.
Bewildered, rebellious, the people grumbled; then
    from God's wilderness came full nourishment for
    the homeward journey.
We will not die, Father Moses said; we will not die
    because Yahweh provides.
This is the bread which the Lord has given; the Holy
    One bestows an amount sufficient to the day.
Father Moses said: Yahweh provides the sufficient
    amount. Take and eat what is enough for today;
    then you shall never lack.

Rescue us, Redeemer God, from solemn captivity.
Free us from the devouring, seductive beast of illusion.

Have pity on us now as you did in the days of Moses.
    You have declared yourself Advocate of the slave
    and Defender of the outcast.
Why have you allowed the exploiters and plunderers to
    triumph, O God? Why do rulers and generals
    stain the pages of history with innocent blood?

Have you forgotten your indelible covenant with
  creation, your promise to heal always the torment
  and woe of your people?

Once again, O Holy One, bring manna from Mystery;
  rain bread upon our guilty streets; feed us who
  have become entangled in the thicket of hatred
  and oppression.
Break apart the gates of illusion; release our
  imprisoned hopes and our half-shaped dreams.
Then shall we stand on the threshold of faith, and
  gather food sufficient to the day.
We will taste the honey flavor of God's Word, and
  come at last victorious out of this vast and jealous
  land.

We will not die, Father Moses said; we will not die
  because Yahweh provides.
Yahweh provides the sufficient amount. Take and eat
  what is enough for today; then you shall never
  lack.

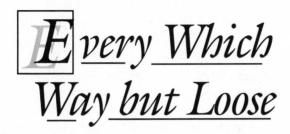

Every Which Way but Loose

Yahweh our God is Sovereign! Let earthly power
　　bow down in the presence of God.
The universe cries out, "Hosanna!" Each particle of
　　matter shouts, "Save us, O Ruler of All!"

Free and holy is the Name of our God! In houses of
　　prayer and in desert places, Yahweh appears; upon
　　mountaintops and in the mean streets have we
　　seen the Lord.
God our Redeemer takes the part of the poor; Yahweh
　　protects those who are physically or mentally
　　disabled.
Give honor to God, and God alone; bring before the
　　Holy One all praise and lament.
There is nothing that cannot be heard by the Giver of
　　Life; Yahweh is like a woman listening for the
　　cries of her newborn child.

O Source of Peace, when we become ensnared by sin,
　　you liberate us; with a mighty hammer you smash
　　our idols of consumption and greed.

Your truth illuminates the scarred bodies of those we
have persecuted; the world's forgotten victims you
keep ever before us.

We travel in your urgent and holy presence! The visible
glories of Unseen Power, the cloud and the fire,
obscure the clamor of evil!

Wherever we go, Yahweh is present. We cannot shake
loose of the covenant-promise.

Holy and free is the Mother who gave us life; steadfast
in love is the King of glory.

All creation pays homage to you, O Sustainer-
Redeemer; people and planets, angels and
animals, all sing out with salvation-voice.

You have numbered us among your saints; let us reject
old loyalties and follow the free and holy God.

Come and worship the Holy One; praise God who is
Ultimate Sovereign!

Let each world resonate to Hope-made-flesh! Let
every dimension echo with the sound of
redemption begun!

Wherever we go, God is present: the Author of Justice
and Defender of the Powerless.

The universe cries out, Hallelujah! From every particle
of matter comes the shout, Praise be to Yahweh!

Sanctuary

You, O God, provide refuge in times of tyranny; you
give us sanctuary from the world's abusive ways.
Your everlasting mercy is the soil in which we take
root; all life is sustained by Ultimate Purpose.
When we are lost, you are the lighthouse that guides
us; you are like the ancient caves that offer shelter
to nomadic shepherds.
In your presence is our dwelling place, a harbor that is
always open, always secure. Because you are God,
we can never be cast adrift.

Before this planet began its orbit, before life emerged
from the primeval mist, you, O Holy One,
claimed the universe as your own.
You are the mother who feeds and protects her
children; you are the hurricane that crashes
against the forces of evil.

We are, all of us, creatures of dust: ephemeral and
broken and bewildered in the presence of Utter
Mystery.

Like the fish of the sea, we see only the present
danger; we are blind to the environment that
gives us life.

You, O Yahweh, encompass both bitter and sweet; you
are the Destroyer and the Preserver, the Journey
and the End.

On this, our Exodus journey, you go ever before us. In
the annealing fire of tragedy and in the fragrant
cloud of grace have you revealed yourself.

Out of this flickering mortal moment, we presume to
call upon you: You are the One who rides
through the desert, riding without limit and
without restraint.

Be true to your promise, O Lord; remember the
covenant you made with our mothers and fathers.

Bring us once again into a fertile, uninjured land; plant
us on your holy mountain.

Dust and water and blood do not define us; your
power alone grants wholeness and value.

Do not hold yourself back from us, O Sustainer of All;
we are the people who bear your holy Name.

Let your judgment fall upon the treachery and hate
that hold Earth captive. Do not allow evil to
destroy this blue-green island in the ocean of
space.

Let our children's children inherit a world crowned by
Justice and ruled by Wisdom. Let them see a time
when the weak are served by the strong, and the
outcasts are no longer outcast.
Empowered and sanctified by your creative Word,
generation after generation will sing your Name!

You, O God, are a sure and certain habitation, a refuge
from evil and a jubilant sanctuary, a place of
belonging and of glory revealed.
In your presence is our dwelling place, a harbor that is
always open, always secure. Because you are God,
we can never be cast adrift!

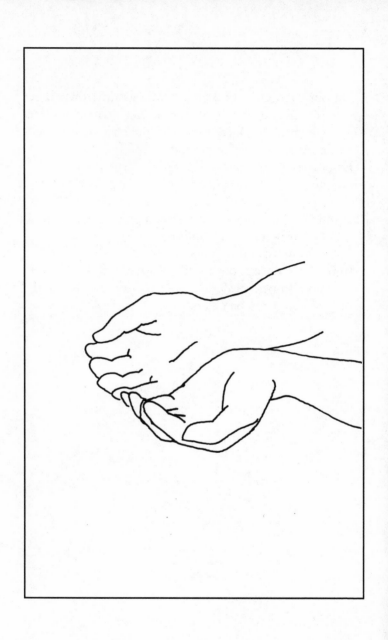

That the World Might Know

How long, O Holy One? How long will you be
   silent?
How long will you resign me to the hungry ravenings
   of destruction? How long before despair hardens
   about me like walls of pearl?

From the midst of garbage cans and broken glass I
   bring my complaint. The decay of poverty and
   hopelessness breeds violence everywhere around
   me.
My ears are filled with the smooth speech of the
   privileged; the world crumbles into particles,
   falling each hour moribund from my hands.

Upon endless, blood-stained pavements my children
   are condemned to wander. Sojourners in a land of
   dark machines, they see with leaden, grief-weary
   eyes.
Impious, mundane death stalks those whose hope has
   dissolved, melted, like grimy fragments of ice. Of
   your silence, O God, repent.

Deliver me from this wild and sad confusion of days;
release me from the bondage of foul and
clamorous nights.
Remember the promise that you made to our mothers
in the wilderness; do not forget the Word with
which you comforted our fathers when they
lamented.

Because you, the Source of All, are one God, I will not
despair.
You see the heart of the mortal world, and open the
eyes of all creation.
You pity the sojourner, and restore those whose lives
have been shattered.

In your faithfulness have I trusted; from beyond space
and time you have heard my cry.
Though death hovers above the place where I sleep,
though my children have been stolen by the
restless and terrible streets,
Yet will I sing: Arise! Awake!
That the world might know whose hand rests upon it;
that the sad and violent world might finally know.
You have snatched us from the furnace of affliction, O
God, and the universe resounds with your
unshakable, jubilant Word.

Exodus

*E*ach night we sleep within bare-earth chambers; like
    rats we dig holes in the hostile ground.
By the anxious light of campfires we tell stories of
    escape; how many years have we traveled without
    ever arriving!
We do not dare count the cost because the cost is too
    high; there is never enough.

Do not forget the refugees, O God; give protection to
    the exiles.
We are like leaves at the mercy of the wind, clumped in
    the gutters of wealthy nations.

From the sudden intrusion of soldiers we fled;
    watching, we saw our fathers gunned down, our
    daughters violated.
Bullets debased the houses we had built: Roofs
    exploded and walls crumbled under the terrific
    force of oppression.
Month after month have we lived in secret, hiding
    from the sound of doors kicked in, shutting our
    ears to the cries of the dead.

Do not forget the refugees, O God; give protection to
    the exiles.

We are like leaves at the mercy of the wind, clumped in
the gutters of wealthy nations.

We are exhausted with running; our bodies still bleed
from the loss of our land and the death of our
dignity.
Aliens in this alien place, we compete with a million
others for beans and rice; we live in perpetual debt
to our rescuers.
Bitterness gnaws upon our rootless lives; we have lived
too long with suspicion and fear.

Give us voice, O Protector of the Helpless; give us
voice to speak for those who are buried in
unmarked graves.
Do not overlook us because we live in the dirt, your
people who inhabit caves and cardboard houses.
Return us to the verdant land of our birth, restore the
freedom that once was ours.

Once more, O Lord, crack open the desert rock, that
your living waters might cleanse us;
Baptize us in the mysterious, protective waters of your
covenant-love.
You are God of the downtrodden and God of the
undeserving, you alone have the power to deliver.
Do not forget the refugees, O God; give protection to
the exiles.

Crossing
the Border

Sing with glorious, intemperate voice! Shout on
    behalf of those who are silent!
Join in uproarious, lyrical movement; dance for the
    ones whose limbs are still!
Proclaim to all nations a bold and a holy truth! Make
    the whole air vibrate with Living Story.
Already the realm of God is begun! The new creation
    has taken its faltering infant steps!

God our Redeemer is one God! It is Yahweh who brings
    about life; it is Yahweh who demands every death.
Turn to the Lord in awe and thanksgiving; honor the
    One who conceived and gave birth to the world!
Seek God in the midst of life; reach out to those who
    are merely existing.

This very day we are chosen; in this awe-filled
    moment, Yahweh's spotlight falls upon us.
Agents of God, we are the ones chosen to care for
    creation; imperfect servants, we are anointed by
    Yahweh to administer justice and love.

Let the frail and downtrodden rejoice! Those who rely
upon the Holy One will be lavished with freedom.
Where Mystery and limitation collide, at the outer
borders of human truth, there does faith abound.
Beyond the boundaries of knowing, we are known;
outside of seeking, we are found.

Yahweh our God is a free God; it is the Holy One who
restores life, who rescues the hopeless and
comforts those who mourn.
God is Sovereign over all. No power can conquer
Yahweh, no evil will defeat our God.

Let us gather into one congregation! Let us offer all
that we have and all that we are to Almighty God!
With singing and music and art and dance, we will
form a living psalm!
Join color to color, word upon word, until the planet
itself resounds with praise!
With paintbrush and canvas, extol the Lord! With
drums and trumpets, tell of the fierce-glowing
hope of the faithful!
The gift of each life is embraced by Yahweh! Already
the realm of God is begun!

Time Is Melting

As tumultuous as a hurricane, as tranquil as a deep
mountain lake is Yahweh's covenant-love.
Unboundable, outreaching, Holy Love embraces
creation.
Every particle of time, each fragment of space reveals
the Godhead; in atoms and in constellations do
we recognize Eternal Meaning.

Those who are jaded and numb reject the call of
Yahweh; what they cannot see, what they cannot
touch, they discard.
They put their trust in the tangible; they fill their
homes with symbols of earthly power.
To false gods they pledge allegiance; to materialism do
they dedicate their lives.
The famous and infamous alike are worshiped; homage
is paid to celebrities as though they had the power
to grant immortality.
Ignoring God's ancient demand for justice, my people
turn away from the poor; with business magnates
and military leaders they have allied themselves.

They tune out the cries of the ragged ones; they avoid
  meeting the gaze of those who keep their
  belongings in shopping carts.

Unable to live in God's holy wilderness, my brothers
  and sisters build vast mansions; they carry their
  property like shields against the onslaught of
  death.
Their professions are deified, and families are sacrificed
  on the altars of visible success.
In a tame, domesticated church, they worship; the
  impassive god of religion demands no
  commitment and offers no challenge.
I grieve when I hear the chant of my people: "What is,
  is what ought to be. What is, is what will be
  forever.
One person cannot change the world; a single human
  gesture does not matter."

Every idol wears a skin of cynicism; each is stuffed with
  dead ideas and poisonous promises.
These gods are created by men and women rushing
  toward annihilation; my people are being
  devoured by their own creations.
Year after year the desperate ones grasp after meaning,
  but all they encounter is the sour, mocking breath
  of implacable decay.

O sisters and brothers, do not make a pact with death;
  reject your treaty with hell.

Every illusion, every imagined security will be smashed
on the rocks of Ultimate Reality. Evil will fall
under the undiminished momentum of divine
purpose.
The Holy One has decreed each life to be of ultimate
significance; the slightest human gesture affects
the universe!

God is so near—so near that you can feel the residue
of hope upon your outstretched arms.
God is so far—so Totally Other that earthly time
breaks under the stress of divine forgiveness.
Our debts have been settled and our sins washed clean;
only through Yahweh's gracious intervention are
we set free.
In the end, it is God who wipes away all tears; it is
God who carries us to safety as a lifeguard rescues
a drowning child.

The bonds of death have shivered apart! Destroy your
idols, put away your pale fears!
To God belong the spinning galaxies and invisible
darkness! Let us raise our voices in praise to the
Holy One, the Mother of Creation, the Father of
All!

Atonement

*I*n the smooth, radiant coolness of early light, I draw
near to the house of God.
Confidence and hope wrap around me like a
transcendent garment, like a coat of many colors.
Peace is my companion; fear no longer rules my heart.

Know that the Holy One will not fail you; through
every terror-drenched night, the Comforter keeps
watch.
From the stranglehold of despair will you be delivered;
God will shield you from the onrush of sorrow.
You will be lifted on the wings of divine compassion;
Yahweh's vigilant care will secure you.

Do not be overcome by anxiety; you are the beloved
of God, an inheritor of the kingdom.
Yahweh will not overlook the vulnerable ones; God
will not reject those who have been brutalized or
afflicted.
When you are caught in the furious waters of adversity,
you will be rescued; the Almighty is your sure and
certain anchor, your indestructible mooring.

From intensive-care units and prisons, Yahweh does
     not turn aside; God hears every word formed by
     weakened lips.
The child who makes her way through gang-ridden
     streets is under God's protection; every lonely,
     perilous place has been declared holy.
There is no life apart from Yahweh; God alone, only
     God, is the Source of all fulfillment, all rest, all
     joy.

Claim for yourself the courage to be; Yahweh has
     known your particular grief, God has atoned for
     all your guilt.
In the midst of human failure, as mortality admits
     defeat, God's banner advances to ultimate victory.
From the midst of a rag-tag army of saints, the Holy
     One calls to you: "Press on, my perfect, imperfect
     note in the symphony of redemption!"

At the moment of death you will not be orphaned; you
     are held by the free and abiding hand of God.
God will convey you through the final corridor;
     through swirling, harmonious light will you
     travel.
At the moment of death you will not be abandoned.
     Within time, beyond time, God is for you; for
     ever and ever God will be with you! Amen.

The Burning Bush

G ive glory to God! Recall the indomitable story of
our mothers and fathers.
Recount the continuing salvation-news; hold fast to
the memory that calms every torment.

To Moses, the sojourner, God's Name was revealed: a
Name so holy we tremble before it.
"I am who I am," the Holy One said. Out of endless
flame God said, "I will become who I will
become."
Like lightning, Yahweh's Word enlivened the sky; pure
Being made sacred the earthly realm.
Rising out of eternity, the Name entered the world,
tearing away illusion, destroying deceit.

Let the panorama of time unite in worship! Let each
historical moment acknowledge our God!
There is no corner of space from which Yahweh is
absent, no *where* that cannot be energized by
divine grace.
Let swamps and deserts, towns and cities rejoice! God
is breathing courage into an exhausted people.

The Word of creation swells above the clatter of earth;
    the faithful still hear the sound of a tree in flames.
Divine syllables are shaping themselves anew;
    wondrous new creatures are formed each day.

Where shall I stand to view infinity? Can my mind put
    bounds around the Almighty?
How shall I take the measure of space? What wisdom
    can encompass the breadth of Mystery?

The Holy One summons creation to repentance;
    justice is God's demand.
From the center of a crumbling tenement house,
    Yahweh roars: "Release the free people of a free
    God!"
Out of a mushroom cloud, the Word judges the earth:
    "Open the gates, tear down every wall of
    separation!
Cut away each strand of barbed wire! Let my people
    go free!"

The Shaper of History declares: "The first shall be last,
    and the last shall be first."
To the helpless will be given shelter, but the
    worshipers of privilege shall feed on ashes.
Humble obedience shall be lifted up, but judgment
    will visit those who ignore the poor.

Let God's Name emblazon every barren place! Impart
    to each generation the continuing, cosmic story!
Reclaim the memory of a forgiven people! Magnify
    Yahweh with exuberant voice!

Medal of Honor

*H*ear, O God, the ungodly torment of a shattered
man.
Each day is like a fist clenching on emptiness; every
night is as sharp and final as a bayonet.
I am condemned to wander like an iceberg adrift in
the Arctic Ocean, the disinherited veteran of an
unclaimable war.
Do not withhold your peace any longer, O Creator of
Mystery; do not abandon me to a nest of death.

Torn from a clear, untasted future, I became part of
the endless column, a partner of dusty tanks and
armored personnel carriers.
I was swept into a nameless, festering conflict. Witness
to the slaughter of innocents, I became the pawn
of decision-makers who dwelled in air-
conditioned quarters a thousand miles away.
Home again, spared from the bullet and the mine, I
encountered a bitter truth: Somewhere in that
alien, smoldering land, my birthright had been
lost.
Some threw flowers at the returning soldiers, most
threw mud and dung.

Legions of fighting men came home; discredited
 heroes all, their tomorrows sealed with blood.

Now I spy on others' lives like a hungry child, like one
 who presses his face against the window of an all-
 night diner.
Beneath the emptiness is more emptiness. I have no
 corpse to bury, and yet I am paralyzed with
 mourning.
Huddled in the corner of my stained, disfigured room,
 I cry out for the life I cannot live: for the marriage
 I cannot have, for the children who are forever
 strangers.

The world has been dismantled by clashing values and
 shattered sanity; human compassion has rusted
 and crumbled.
Why did you spare my life, O God, only to consign me
 to a more terrible hell?
Have you made yourself known to the prisoner, but
 closed your ears to my bitter prayers?
Shunned by all, I am a dying man; I possess nothing;
 nothing can I lose.
Though this be my final breath, O God, I will not
 keep silence. You must listen to the cry of a
 downtrodden, vanquished man.
You must hear your servant, O Holy One; you cannot,
 you will not, abandon me to the answerless void.
For you are at work in the darkness as well as the light;
 you have chosen all creation to be your beloved.

We are forever bound to you, the Ruler of Time and
Space, and you have declared yourself to be the
enduring covenant-partner of every creature.

Do not allow the hollow echo of my voice to be the
only living reply to this anguish! Remember your
promise of redemption.
Do not leave me careering on a carnival ride gone out
of control! Deliver me, O God, from the rage and
the outrage of a peaceless, unheeded death.

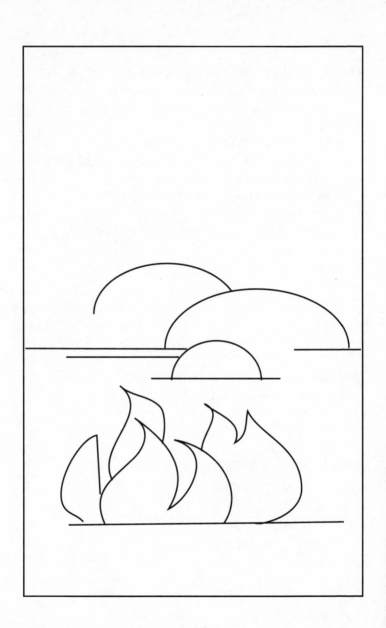

*E*piphany

*B*lessed be God: Creator, Redeemer, Sustainer. And
blessed be the One who forgives our sins.

We stand in the holy presence of saints; with our
fathers and mothers, we bear witness to your
glory.

Let all the living who have ever lived join hands with
the children who are yet to be. Let prophets and
martyrs, healers and preachers, draw near to the
throne of grace.

We have been called to a holy purpose; before time
and space, we were claimed by Living God.

Ours is a bold and a perilous mission: to carry faith
into the midst of evil, to oppose injustice with
love, to overturn apathy with shouts of hope.

For freedom, we have been set free; the Holy One has
already paid the bitter ransom.

Listen and heed the Word of God: "When did you call
that I did not answer? When did you weep that I
was not there?

In the desert I cracked open the rock that you might
drink. With salvation-light I have shattered the
bondage of death.

With fire and cloud have I led you; my covenant goes
before you as beacon and guide.

"Pay attention, my forgetful people. Do not submit
yourselves to slavery.
Do not listen to the easy words of mortal gods; put
nothing in the place of wilderness faith.
Honor the creation: be good stewards of body and
mind; respect the earth and its marvelous
creatures.
Be vigilant against the demons of envy. Grace
bestowed upon another is always grace imparted
to you.
Speak the truth; do not inflict harm by falsehood or by
silence.
Harbor no malice or hatred; seek justice and freedom
for all creation.

"Repent, my beloved. Let your hearts respond to the
unfading comfort of my Word.
Be alert, as one who waits to hear a familiar footstep.
There is no moment when I am far off, no time
when I am absent.
Your wrongdoing I have set aside, and I have erased
your sin."

Listen to the Word that liberates; hear the good news
that nourishes every hungry child:
"Though my people disobey, I will not forsake them.
I am their steadfast teacher; their judge and their
strength.

With compassion I will shelter all creatures, from the
    smallest to the largest.
Not one will be lost from the holy and infinite caravan,
    the caravan of God that is traveling, full-glorious
    and infinite and free, into the dawn of redemption
    day."

No Other Moment

*B*lessed be God, Ruler of Time and Space! Yahweh
kindles the light of justice and hallows the plight
of the helpless.
Every living creature is sacred and chosen; each one is
Yahweh's special possession.

From the ashes of Mystery the Holy One calls forth
prophets; God calls young and old, male and
female, healthy and infirm, to preach the Word of
life.
Wisdom has sent her prophets into the withered air of
boardrooms and into secret underground
chambers; they are teachers and mechanics and
parents and preachers.
With relentless faith the messengers of Yahweh speak
out; they will not be silenced.
To the strong and to the poor are the prophets sent;
they announce the triumph of holiness over the
subtle power of death.

Let the call to worship be sounded! Let guitars and
tambourines, tympani and strings, join in
refulgent praise!

Weave together the voices of tuba and flute, organ and
cymbal; join every instrument into the expanding
symphony!
Then shall the outer reaches of space echo with
awakened song! The universe is waiting on tiptoe
for us to abandon our fears!
There is no other moment, no other time; now is our
time to live and our time to worship!

Let the rude, obscene noises of war dissolve into
reverent silence; then let the world's children lead
this bleeding, burdened world in a thunderous
song of amaze!
Let every city vibrate with life, pulsing to the eternal
heartbeat at its core.
Let the stars form constellations of praise, while
humanity feeds the darkness with particles of
visible sound.
Stand back and listen to the forests rejoice! Hear the
harmony of waterfalls and the euphony of
canyons!

Sound the call to worship! Embrace this moment of
wholeness, abandon every fear!
Yahweh our God is one God! There is no other
moment; no other time to live and to worship the
Lord!

Let the Name of God burst forth, explode, and erupt!
Let all creation join together in one holy, living
shout:
"Hallelujah! Hallelujah to the Lord of Hosts!"

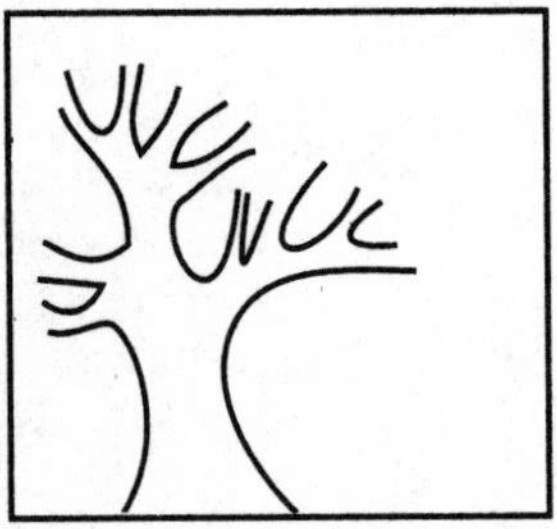

Tiger, Tiger

All creation is lush with God; Wisdom embraces
　　everything that dies and lives!
The Holy One governs the sweeping movement of
　　constellations; each bewildered creature dwells
　　within the circle of Yahweh's vigilant care.

Let every woman and man bear witness: The realm of
　　God approaches; it is drawing very near indeed!

Like an untamed animal that is running, breathing
　　rapidly, the kingdom bears down upon creation.
Let every child and adult sing loud: "Yahweh it is who
　　inverts the world's values!"
The God of the prophets denounces bigotry; the God
　　of Paul and Peter uplifts those who are called
　　unfit.

Standing in the splendid company of the poor, and in
　　the presence of the misbegotten, we rejoice!
Cruelty and injustice will not be tolerated; God is
　　victorious over sin!
To us has been revealed the Hallelujah-news: We are
　　God's children; we are inheritors of abundant life.

151

In spite of malice, in spite of atrocity, the Holy One
will not withhold salvation.
Evil is not immortal; it cannot turn back the
oncoming, jubilant tide of divine purpose!

See! The realm of God approaches; it is stalking an
unsuspecting, unrepentant universe.

Human time is melting; the frail structures of
chronology are giving way under the terrible
stress of God's time.
Even now we are tasting the first fruits of that which is
to come; even now upon our faces we feel the
gracious summer rain.
Yahweh's final triumph is so close, so forever present;
surely we shall touch eternity before the intake of
another breath!

Already the realm of God has arrived; but the realm of
God is not yet fulfilled!

Shout your loud and raucous faith: God alone, is
ultimate; only God!
One virtue alone has meaning in this time-between-
the-times: only humble acknowledgment of God!
One sin alone begets all others: the pride that denies
God's absolute sovereignty!
Humble acknowledgment honors God; and obedience
springs from reverence.
As a child nurses at the breast, we draw nourishment
from divine forgiveness.

By choosing life instead of death, we affirm Yahweh's
    creative purpose. Only faith can overcome apathy!

When God has given so much, why do we scramble for
    the first seat? Why do we seek the place of highest
    honor?
Why do we demand more and more and more? Shall
    we forever presume upon the goodness of God?
All creation has been invited; at the banquet all will be
    seated without rank or position.

Because Yahweh has paid the blood ransom, we are
    freed from the lethal grip of fear.
Abused children, addicted adults, outcasts, and
    strangers: These are they who will be summoned
    to God's nearer favor.
Arriving at long last in the Holy Presence, these are
    they who will hear, with wonder and vivid amaze:
Blessed are the frightened ones who have reached their
    limits; blessed are the lonely and the suicidal.
Blessed are the spiritually poor; blessed are those who
    place what little is left of reliance and faith upon
    the Holy One.

Already the realm of God has arrived; but the realm of
    God is not yet fulfilled!

Choose today whom you will serve! In this hovering,
    vibrant moment, every creature must decide for
    life or for death.

Will faith or unfaith write your epitaph? Will heaven or
hell design your days?

Yahweh shakes the world loose of lies and pretensions!
The Holy One is casting demons out of creation!
Sing a new song of transforming grace! Raise your
voices in splendid praise!
Into a vast, effulgent whirlwind, the Ruler of History
is gathering creation! All of life and all of time are
spinning with divine purpose!

The realm of God approaches; it is drawing very near
indeed!

Free at Last

Yahweh is Sovereign over all! Assign to God full
   glory and praise!
Let every creature acknowledge Holy Presence; let
   spinning atomic particles worship the Source of
   Life.
Deaf children will hear the Holy Word, and the
   sightless ones will see the Promise-made-flesh.
Those who have died are alive to God! We are all
   living sons and daughters of Yahweh.

Like a consuming fire, the Spirit of God blazes forth,
   saving the world from its own depravity.
Fierce and wolflike, God restores peace to every
   troubled spirit; Yahweh has declared solidarity
   with the outcast and with the poor.
Using the hesitant, staggering movement of history,
   God is at work redeeming the world; divine
   energy breaks down every closed border!
Not one strand of barbed wire shall remain! The
   foundations of evil have been shaken and shaken!

Over the disappearing rain forests, the Holy One
   hovers; God it is who protects the rivers and
   shelters the fragile nighthawk.

In the solitary reaches of space, God is still at work,
   spinning clouds of hydrogen; unformed galaxies
   are even now coalescing, condensing, into living
   light.
Without ceasing, the saints testify to overwhelming
   Mystery; they proclaim the free, uncontainable
   God!
Without ceasing, the saints bear witness to the melting
   of hatred, to the groaning and cracking of
   intolerance!
Cheering and dancing across eternity, the saints give
   praise to the Holy One who triumphs over evil;
   they sing and they dance as war dissolves into
   rain!

The smallest human gesture is valued by the Almighty;
   from all of life Yahweh forges salvation.
The God of Wholeness, the Sovereign of Space-Time,
   will not be denied! Covenant-power is our
   strength, our inheritance!
Shouting Hallelujah, we, too, will dance across the
   border! We, too, will enter a realm without guards
   or tunnels or towers!
We are all of us traveling with the saints, traveling in
   God's holy caravan of eternal purpose and
   amazing grace! Rejoicing, we will somersault
   across the no-time of eternity!

The Winding Path

What right do you have, O humanity; what right do
you have to clothe yourself in the skins of your
victims?

Why do you turn your back on your holy birthright?
Have you forgotten the promise and demand of
covenant-love?

Invisible poisons billow into a once-immaculate sky,
and radiation settles in our veins like sediment at
the bottom of a river.

Seals and whales and elephants perish; these are the
casualties of human greed.

Creature after creature entrusted to your care stands
on the brink of extinction. The planet is
convulsed with death.

Remember, my people, that there is no escape from
the love of God; even now the Holy One stalks
the earth.

Those who ravage the helpless cannot hide from the
Judge of All; the unrighteous will be baptized
with tears and ashes.

Temples dedicated to security, the stock exchanges and
the banks, cannot stand against Yahweh; a sudden
wind will carry away the debris of racism and
exploitation.

Even the house of God has been corrupted, its light
obscured by weak words and false piety.
The Lord's house has become an ice-coated tower, a
refuge from the roar of the lion; my people have
created false sanctuary against the snarling of the
Lord of Life.

But Yahweh will not be denied; the universe echoes
with the thunder of mercy about to be unleashed.
The world's armed indifference cannot survive the
headwind of Mystery; murderous contempt and
savage blindness will not endure.
As for me, I have put my faith in the hurtling freedom
of God, my trust in Yahweh's deliverance.
Divine fire will once again ignite the power of the
Spirit, and God's people will reclaim their
discarded heritage.
Because we are the redeemed and the stewards of
creation, we are called to resist every harsh and
brooding evil.

I give thanks for the nourishing vortex of Wisdom. I
rejoice in the unshackled Hallelujah-force of
covenant-love.

Like a dream before my eyes, I see my people
    embracing God's triumphant *yes!* I see an
    awakened people entering the bright,
    unshadowed garden of salvation.

The Suffering Streets

*F*irst came once-worded, awful Creator-*yes!* Then the
  nothing that was, erupted into *all* and *now.*
Morning's extravagant light was bonded to evening;
  God's primeval darkness took its place in the
  company of the redeemed.
Then, from original dust, God wove thick ribbons of
  planets and stars and sub-atomic particles.
  Creation Day tumbled forward and backward and
  outward.
And the Word was with God, holding God: weeping,
  dreaming, laughing, shouting for joy,
While Wisdom, in dreadful, cosmic groaning, gave
  birth to human passion. Acting in full freedom,
  Yahweh bestowed freedom upon the world.

In these broken days of greed and decay, who can
  recapture an untainted life? Can a flower recede
  into the bud?
Earth is strangled by chaos and crushed by
  blasphemous wars. Who in this failing world can
  know the presence of God?

To those who wrestle with death, life shall be given.
Wholeness comes to those who follow God into
the suffering streets.
Blessing is bestowed upon women and men who give
shelter to the abused; those who overturn cruelty
are called righteous.
Both young and old bear witness to the relentless love
of God; these will breathe the rinsed, immaculate
air of infinity.

Where human finitude reaches its outer limits, there
does the Spirit surround us; by Holy Mystery we
are sustained.
Where life is no longer trivialized and coercion puts
down its weaponry, the Word rings out with
eternal newness.
Where hostages are freed and rivers purified, there you
will see the outskirts of the realm of God.

Sound the alarm of peace! Everything that lives is
holy!
Breaking into history from eternity, the wolf howls and
howls; the bear rises up to defend her creation.
Let us delight in God's unfinished work: the divine
caravan of empty and full, beauty and terror,
morning and evening.

Sound the alarm of peace! Everything that lives is
holy!

Let every ocean shed the tarnish of oil! Let oxygen
    radiate from the hallowed rain forests!
The Source of All has bestowed upon us a second
    chance; right now God is opening our eyes to the
    hidden things.

In the presence of myriad stars, Yahweh summons
    humankind; God is commissioning us to pulsating
    new life.
Bandage the wounds of vengeance! Gather a harvest of
    extravagant, riotous dreams!
Let us come together and shout, "Glory to the Lord!
    Glory to God who created and still is creating!
    Glory to the Lord! Glory to the Lord! Amen!"

Razzle-Dazzle

*S*ing Hallelujah! Sing to the Lord!
Shout with joy in the presence of Wisdom!

Start with the loud and the stalwart drum; brushes on
    cymbals, sibilant whispering.
Then add piano and bass and chimes, ribbons of cello
    to sing of the Savior.
Let all creation unite in the song! Tell of the Holy
    One; sing loud of Yahweh.

All have strayed from the ways of peace; sin has
    entangled us, every one.
But God has triumphed! Publish the news! Yahweh has
    conquered the forces of evil.
Not a sparrow shall fall, not a child shall stumble; each
    one is held by the hand of God.

Sing of life and God-worded freedom! Death cannot
    hinder the train of salvation.
Transformed by *yes,* and delivered from *no;* we are the
    children of rainbow-promise.

Let trumpet and oboe and bugle rejoice; give praise
with heart and mind and voice.

Give thanks to the Holy One! Shout Amen!
Sing Hallelujah to God forever!

ilderness

G lory to you, O Giver of Peace! Glory to you,
Redeemer of All!
Out of the inmost depths of life, I call upon the holy
Name of God; every anguished mortal breath
engenders the giving of thanks.

Hear my words, O covenant people: Do not seek
safety in earthly power.
Security lies only in the holy insecurity of God.
Governments cannot triumph except in their own
destruction.
Like buildings destroyed by a terrible earthquake,
every empire will collapse into rubble; nothing
shall remain.

Fulfilled is she who places her confidence in God, the
Passionate Advocate and Infinite Mystery; her
delight is always in the paths of justice.
Truly human is he who perceives the bright image of
eternity in the faces of the poor; his trust is in
God and God alone.
Yahweh takes the part of all those whose lives are
constricted by the barbed wire of racism.

And to those who are fleeing oppression, the Holy
    One gives safe harbor.
God is the guardian of the ones whom the world calls
    limited, those who hold fast to the trust and
    courage of childhood.
It is God who enters the schools where weapons and
    drugs hold sway; it is Yahweh who raises up
    teachers and principals and students to shake off
    the demons of apathy.

The Creator roars without ceasing when the privileged
    ones wallow in surplus goods. God judges a world
    that watches drought victims languish while
    waiting for promised food.
Nor will Yahweh allow the universe to forget a night
    when thousands upon thousands of windows were
    shattered; the Almighty will not ignore the
    unhealed cruelty that made way for death in the
    gas chambers.

Earthly shackles do not bind the Holy One; nor does
    Immortal God tremble.
The Judge of All will not let us pronounce our own
    death sentence; the One who rides in the desert
    emerges full-glorious to quench the fires of
    condemnation.
Breathing life into ravaged bones, God's furious
    headwind calls us again to faithfulness as a
    covenant people.

From blighted streets and from rose-shadowed
mountaintops we will shout: "Yahweh be
praised!"
From everlasting to everlasting, Yahweh gathers all
creation into redemption, enlivening the universe
with holy, triumphant, unstifled grace!

 Yahweh Saves

When the angel of death spared their children, a
    people in slavery rejoiced.
Uncertain and free, the people stepped forward;
    through parted waters they passed unharmed.
With faith as their shield, they entered the wilderness;
    the path of uncertainty became their way.

When palm branches covered the road and stones cried
    out Hosanna, the world was rocked by Truth.
When palm branches covered the road and stones cried
    out Hosanna, armies were routed and evil took
    flight.
Chronology splintered and shackles were broken;
    creation took a new and a frightened breath.

When the veil of the temple was split, when death
    shrieked with the pangs of death,
When the headwind of God passed over the earth, into
    one moment was history condensed.
Humility overturned the rule of the arrogant; grace
    was bestowed on the weak and forsaken.

The taste of salvation lingered like wine; we saw, but
we did not understand.

Tell me, my people: Can you discern from whence you
came? Can you show me your destination?
Can you explain the mystery of life? Can you calculate
the limits of the universe?
Remember, O creation, that you are dust, and to dust
you shall return.
Remember, O creation, that you are free, and to
freedom you are called.
We are the colleagues of God, Yahweh's chosen
partners.
Trust is our beacon, and obedience our banner.

Listen to the rushing wind of God; every lifeless idol
has been torn apart.
Hear the roar of Incarnate Word; God is at work
reshaping creation.
Spread your cloaks before the Lord, and scatter your
pride on the ancient cobblestones.
Rejoice! Cry Hosanna! Step into freedom and shout:
Hosanna in the highest!